Breaking Through

WELLINGTON BOONE

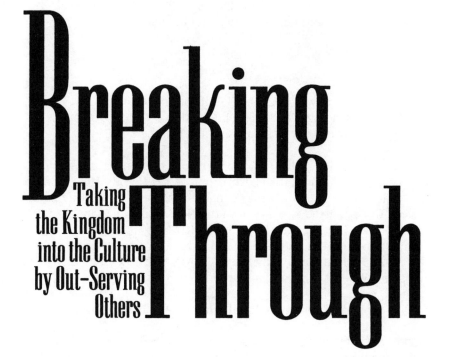

Breaking

Taking
the Kingdom
into the Culture
by Out-Serving
Others

Through

BROADMAN
&HOLMAN
PUBLISHERS

Nashville, Tennessee

Published by:
Broadman & Holman Publishers
Nashville, Tennessee
4253-96
0-8054-5396-2

Dewey Decimal Classification: 248.4
Subject Heading: CHRISTIAN LIFE \ MEN—RELIGIOUS LIFE
Library of Congress Card Catalog Number: 95-26488

Unless otherwise indicated, all Scripture references are from The New King James Version (NKJV), Copyright © 1979, 1980, 1982, Thomas Nelson, Inc., Publisher. References marked KJV are from the King James Version. Those marked NASB are from the New American Standard Bible, © 1960, 1962, 1963, 1968, 1971, 1972, 1973, 1975, and 1977 by The Lockman Foundation, and are used by permission. Other references marked TLB are from The Living Bible, Copyright © 1971, Tyndale House Publishers, Wheaton, Ill., and are used by permission.

Library of Congress Cataloging-in-Publication Data

Boone, William Wellington, 1948–
   Breaking through / William Wellington Boone.
     p.   cm.
   Includes bibliographical references.
   ISBN 0-8054-5396-2
   1. Boone, William Wellington, 1948–   . 2. Afro-American clergy—
Biography. I. Title.
BR563.N4B66   1996
243—dc20

95-26488
CIP

00 99 98 97 96 5 4 3

Contents

This book is dedicated to my loving wife,
Katheryn, my number-one inspiration for
thirty-one years.
Thank you for loving me unconditionally,
standing with me in the trials, and for being
there, second only to the Holy Spirit.

Today's Christian Leaders Speak about Wellington Boone

I appreciate the ministry of Wellington Boone and the vision God has given him. He is a man of conviction and passion for the gospel of Jesus Christ. He is certainly one of the new Christian leaders on the horizon today.

Franklin Graham
President, Samaritan's Purse

Wellington Boone speaks to a generation with words that pierce to the heart of the matter. The power of his message comes from the depths of his commitment to Christ and to those he addresses. I count it a distinct privilege to know Wellington Boone, both as a man of God and as a friend.

Ben Kinchlow
Co-host, 700 Club

America's need today is a call for a coming revival. Revival comes from fasting, praying, and seeking God's face. Wellington Boone is modeling and preaching this mandatory message.

Bill Bright
Founder, Campus Crusade for Christ

Wellington epitomizes the phrase, "Fall on the rock and be broken." Only through brokenness can the fragrance fill the room.

Ricky Skaggs
Rs Entertainment, Inc.

Foreword

*J*esus Christ is coming soon. Christian men and women of all races must rally around the Truth. God's honor is at stake. He has raised up Wellington Boone for such a time as this.

In football, every good signal caller understands the head coach's instructions. He perceives, anticipates, and reacts with precision and daring. For the kingdom of God, Wellington Boone is that man.

I have watched him move in and out of life's difficulties, maintaining his allegiance to Christ with true passion and commitment. His message crosses all racial and cultural barriers. He brings people together for reconciliation and restoration to unity in Christ. With an eternal perspective, Wellington delivers God's vision of liberation from all forms of slavery and tyranny in life.

I love this man.

I have locked hearts with him for the purpose of changing this world.

I trust this man.

His love for God's Word and his burning desire that this generation know Christ shine through his life. Sometimes he is easy to read and sometimes he must be studied carefully. But I exhort you: Take time to read and listen to the message within these pages.

I admire this man.

Wellington is attuned to his Lord. He has a heart that is sensitive to his fellow man. I am always fascinated as I observe how his mind focuses on the piercing truths of God with remarkable consistency. He looks you right in the eye and points to the dictates of divine purpose.

I am in the game with Wellington Boone to bring this generation to Jesus. This book will fill you with vision and courageous insights that take your faith to the next level.

Bill McCartney
Co-founder, Promise Keepers

Acknowledgments

*G*rateful acknowledgment is made to some meaningful people in my life.

Attorney John Deal seeded prophetic vision for our lives into my wife and me when no one else saw us.

Coach Bill McCartney, co-founder of Promise Keepers, for being the most vocal white Christian I have met. He is devoted to reaching the black man and helping him find his creative purpose. He will not be swayed until it happens.

Cynthia Ellenwood, a former executive assistant, for seeding journalism and editorial skills to me as a pioneer.

Gloria Mayo, who has been with me for all these years, doing the myriad things she is called upon to do. She has given her heart and love to making this ministry known, even while working under the most adverse conditions.

My Governmental Eldership—Garland Hunt, Brian Crute, Monte Knight, Marvin Mason, and Larry Jackson—for sending me out to the nations to reach the generation while wanting, loving, and needing me on the local level.

Richard P. Rosenbaum Jr., editorial director for Broadman & Holman Publishers, for staying after me for two years to do this book with them and not being offended with the countless delays in my selection process. He has proved himself as someone who sees the message I have more than just selecting a new author.

Sarah Coleman, journalist, for working with me to refine this message and for her prayers and vigilance in seeing to it that I met my deadline and, most importantly, wrote the heart of Jesus.

Kin Clinton, for being more than a manager—a friend I love and one I am thrilled to have covenanted with.

I acknowledge you all with a host of others, well known to the Lord, who have sown seeds of His life and love into my life.

Wellington Boone

1

Are You Hungry?

As the hart panteth after the water brooks, so panteth my soul after thee, O God. My soul thirsteth for God, for the living God: when shall I come and appear before God?

Psalm 42:1–2, KJV

No living person can escape the desire to eat and drink. In America these two needs are met regularly every day. But there is another kind of hunger and thirst that is rarely satisfied: the hunger for meaning and destiny.

People try to fill the void in many ways. Young and old flock to rock concerts. People sit in front of their televisions during daytime talk shows, searching among the filth for the next thrill. Scores assemble at places like Tiananmen Square, searching for freedom. The final episode of "Cheers" was dubbed a "national disaster." Why? That bar at 127-1/2 Beacon Street in Boston was a place where "everybody knew your name, they treated you the same and were glad you came." It was the one place where for thirty minutes many could suspend reality and belong. There is meaning and fulfillment in belonging, and even though "Cheers" wasn't real, it was as close as many people ever came. No matter how hard we try, we know, deep down, that our false images won't last. Sooner or later we have to give them up and get on with the hard work of living in the real world.

A Search for Meaning

A middle-aged black man on skid row in Los Angeles recently paraded down the street with a sign that read, I NEED 'BREAD' TO GET ME TO THE MILLION MAN MARCH IN D.C. He held out a hat for donations to finance his trip to the 1995 event. Drugs and alcohol had failed; maybe he could fill the void in his heart by going to the march. He, like thousands of others, felt empty but didn't realize that you cannot find meaning in an ocean of lost souls.

This man's father had been in Washington in 1963, gathering with whites and blacks at the Lincoln Memorial with demands to pass civil rights legislation. And those demands were met. But what effect did this victory have for him? His only son was steeped in hate and was imprisoned for "wasting" a rival gang member. Three generations in search of imperishable food, all left empty. His father may have been searching for the right thing, but did he go to the right place to find it?

Few will forget the surge of the crowd when Martin Luther King Jr. made his "I have a dream" speech, accompanied by white folk singers such as Joan Baez and Bob Dylan. One writer described the event as "in keeping with King's color-blind vision of the sons of former slaves and the songs of former slave owners, sitting together to feed at the table of brotherhood." Even today I know few people who can't sit through a recording of that same speech without being captured by the beauty of the vision of a unified country. King's legacy will remain with us, but how many neighborhoods have become brotherhoods? Is this nation closer to judging people by the content of their character? The work has been done in the House of Representatives and the Senate of this great nation, but we have forgotten the greater work that must be done at the altar of repentance. Even with legislative victories, the insatiable hunger for meaning persists.

Rhetoric does not satisfy the soul. New laws will not feed people who are starving for purpose. Only Jesus does. Two thousand years ago He proclaimed that man shall not live by bread alone, but by every word that proceeds out of the mouth of God (Matt. 4:4).

Are you hungry? broken? dispossessed? searching for meaning? purpose? This book is for everyone who has ever marched behind the drummers of discontent. Do you thirst for truth? God wants to speak to you straight from His heart. After hope and reason have failed, faith conquers.

Jeremiah, an Old Testament prophet, said:

Your words were found, and I did eat them, and Your word was to me the joy and rejoicing of my heart.

Jeremiah 15:16

God's word became flesh in Jesus and can become flesh in your life, too. Whether you are a Christian or not, if you are tired of a purposeless life, if you are truly hungry for righteousness, then the Bible has good news for you. The Bible promises that if you are hungry for righteousness you will be filled (Matt. 5:6).

Maybe you've lived so thirsty and hungry for so long, even as a Christian, that you have come to believe you could never be made full again. But the Spirit of God is waiting to blow a fresh breeze of fulfillment right into your life. Jesus has more answers than you have questions, more love than you have needs, and—the best news of all—He deals in the past, the present, and the future!

He Is Lord of the Breaking Through!

By now you've probably heard of the spiritual hunger of the Promise Keepers. You can feel the hunger for God in the tens of thousands of men who gather in stadiums across this nation. It is not uncommon to hear the words, "I've tried everything." "I am unsatisfied." "I need a breakthrough." Men by the thousands have been searching for answers and are making a simple, yet profound, discovery: Jesus has them. An untold number have accepted the rather stringent guidelines of becoming a Promise Keeper. A Promise Keeper is a man committed to honoring Jesus Christ, his wife, his church, and his community.

This movement began with only a handful of men in 1990, but since then it has grown into a worldwide organization. Bill McCartney, former head football coach at the University of Colorado, felt a growing hunger for a deeper walk with God. He soon recognized he wasn't the only one. His words reverberate through stadiums across America: "I believe almighty God has given me a message that will change your life. Forgive and give and you will live!"

Challenging men to measure up to their God-given responsibilities was born in his heart. He had studied the landscape and soon recognized that success and being number one in the ranks of college football did not end his quest for what endures. Confronted with the reality that he was not the "promise keeper" God intended, he started this movement with the express desire of having it model the lifestyle of Jesus.

At the Silver Dome in Detroit, eighty thousand men met with one goal: to become promise keepers under one head, the Lordship of Jesus Christ. These were individuals hungry to become men of substance, making an irrevocable commitment to take God at His word and to be reconciled to God in every area of their lives. If Martin Luther King would have seen that meeting in action, he would have seen his color-blind vision in action.

I join Coach McCartney in his words that "the hope of Promise Keepers is that men would dare to enter into the struggle for righteousness and, shoulder to shoulder, seize this divine opportunity to further the kingdom of God."

When coming onto the platform at Promise Keepers, I talk to the group as if they were one man. It doesn't matter how many needs are represented, Jesus can meet every one of them. The O. J. Simpson trial highlighted the significance of every hair on every head. The Bible declares that God has numbered every hair on your head. They are numbered! Jesus sees you as an individual person, not just one in a sea of humanity.

I am convinced that no man could have orchestrated this move of God. Men's hearts are being touched by God, and they come, hungry to hear His word. In many cases it does not matter who is speaking, because Jesus is speaking through vessels of clay.

God Said . . . You're Right. You Are Inadequate.

I am burdened as Jesus is burdened. Yet many times after sharing my heart, I feel inadequate. At those times, God comes to me and says, "You know, Wellington, you're right. You are inadequate." The surprising thing is, the more inadequate I feel, the greater the impact. God has His way of taking our nothingness and linking it to Almightiness. That is the difference. It is His work, and I am humbled to be a part in reaching out and touching others. My overwhelming desire is to never forget who He is and who I am not!

My prayer is the same for a huge audience of men as for a few who gather together in an inner-city storefront. It is that everyone will catch the vision of destiny and move to higher levels with God.

I remember being in Nashville with some country western singers. There were about twenty-five of us in a room. With me was a good friend, Ricky Skaggs. What a heart he has for God. Meeting with us were two older gentlemen, much like patriarchs in the faith. They came to pray for us and to pass their mantles of faithfulness on to men younger in the Lord. While one of the men was praying over us, it became clear to me that everything he was praying for related directly to me and my needs. I knew it was a corporate prayer, but God was speaking every word to me.

When he finished, Ricky raised his hand and said, "You know, brother, while you were praying for those other guys, it was as if everything you were praying for these other people was mine."

I thought to myself, this guy is trying to be as greedy and hungry for God as I am! I immediately put my hand up and said, "Me, too. I felt the same thing." I was moved by Ricky's heart toward the Lord, and from that point on I was aware he was trying to "outhunger" me. I was not about to let another man be greedier for Jesus than I was! I had to keep an eye on him!

The inspiration of this country western singer gripped my heart. So genuine was his love for God—a true portrait of self-lessness. I was determined to be part of this picture. Sometimes people think prominent people who have won the world's praise are more into money and people than seeking the applause of heaven. While this may be true of others it is certainly not true of Ricky.

The second gentleman gave a word, but noted he felt it was not necessary to pray over us. For a time he shared from his heart and imparted to us Godly wisdom. Suddenly Ricky got up, and the sound of water filling a basin could be heard. Before I knew it, he came around to this man and asked if he could wash his feet. With great dignity, the man took off his shoes, and Ricky quietly began the task. But he only washed one foot because I sprinted for the other one! Ricky was not going to be more humble for God than me. No sir! In a spirit of deep worship we became competitive for God—jealous over who would outserve the other in honoring this dear man. At this point another man joined us and began drying the man's feet. I'm sure this scene caused our God to smile. There we were, grown men, arguing over the feet of one of His saints!

Ricky then took the water away, but I got to put the shoes back on and tie the laces. I recalled the servant heart of Jesus and remembered how He washed the feet of His disciples and His admonition that we should wash one another's feet. Observing this kindly man of God I thought, how beautiful are the feet of them that preach the gospel of peace.

Another significant event transpired after the foot washing. The man of God felt refreshed, and he had it on his heart to pray for us and to lay hands on those of us who washed his feet. For a simple act, we had become recipients of his prayer.

The transference of anointing is seen from Elijah to Elisha, Moses to the seventy, and Paul to Timothy. We got some of that! Yes sir! But do you know what? I'm still hungry for more, for everything God has in store for me.

Why Was I Born?

I believe we are in the end times. I believe I was born into this dark hour to declare the coming of God's kingdom. God has given me faith, and I possess great confidence that God is coming soon. I believe I am one of the ones who has been handpicked and blessed to reach out to a hurting people, to bring them the light, to encourage them beyond their troubles, and to set an example of raising up leaders to go out into every area of life and every field to be salt and light to a dying world. I am called to offer love, not condemnation, and hope, not destruction, and to look at the weakest element of society and prove the reality of God there. I also see those in the world's ivory towers and point out to them that there is something more to life than material abundance, presenting truths from the Bible that life consists of more than the things that a man possesses. For what shall it profit a man to gain the whole world and lose his soul?

Why Were You Born?

It is a sad fact that most Christians don't hear the call of God on their lives. There's something about which we can be very sure: God is calling. That is why I am compelled to ask, Do you hear God's call? God is calling you, right now, to walk in fullness with Him. This world is soon passing and everything in it. God is laying claim to your life, that you might take on the fullness of Christ. We have to ask ourselves, Are we serving God for His hands or His feet? The answer may be the reason our walk with God is less than the abundance He has promised. If you are serving God for His hands, you're serving Him for what you can get, for the blessings He will give. God blesses us all the time, and He will continue to do so. He is our heavenly Father. He loves us, and, more than anyone, He knows how to give good gifts. But being materially and physically blessed of God doesn't say anything about you or me. The gift says nothing about the receiver. You and I can have all our needs met and still be a rebel.

You Can Get Your Needs Met and Still Be a Rebel

Think about the children of Israel. How many times did God meet their needs only to experience again their rebellion? Now it's time for a look in the mirror. We are no different. The gift only speaks of the giver. If we are serving God only for His hands we are self-focused, baby Christians, not ready for solid spiritual food.

God is looking for Christians who will serve Him for His feet. The feet speak of one's walk or lifestyle. God is calling you to model the lifestyle of Jesus Christ. This is why you were born. By modeling Jesus, being conformed to His image, you are preparing to be the bride of a Christ. Through modeling Christ we glorify God here on earth, drawing others to Him. As the bride of Christ, we will enjoy Him forever in eternity.

More than a century ago, in 1857, the birth of a great awakening formed in the heart of Christian businessman, Jeremiah Lampier. He was impressed of God to start noonday prayer meetings with some of his business associates. They met together, and it soon became apparent that God was at work in their individual lives. Their numbers grew, and from that small nucleus, revival fire spread.

The vision of Promise Keepers represents an awesome work of God that resembles the historic awakening in church history. It brings us to the last two verses in the Old Testament:

Behold, I will send you Elijah the prophet before the coming of the great and dreadful day of the LORD. And he will turn the hearts of the fathers to the children, and the hearts of the children to their fathers, lest I come and strike the earth with a curse.

Malachi 4:5–6

If there had been no New Testament, the final word of the Bible would have been a curse. Sin was everywhere, and the need for the coming Messiah became greater than ever. Malachi was calling the people to repentance, and the day of the Lord would reveal it was not vain to serve God.

Like Israel in the days of Malachi, America today is filled with renegade Christians who have reneged on their biblical responsibility in their homes. The evidence is everywhere. As God came to Jeremiah Lampier, so He came also to Bill McCartney and Dave Wardell who asked seventy of their friends to join them in prayer. That meeting never made the network news. It was just an ordinary group of men committed to extraordinary accountability to each other and to serving God with their feet.

I am convinced this last-day move points to the end of the age. The explosion taking place in the lives of these men motivates them to turn their hearts to their children, and the children's hearts are coming toward the fathers. It is what Malachi was talking about.

At times we forget it was a man who failed in the person of Adam. In Jesus Christ, the last Adam, was the God-man who succeeded. Adam tried to hide himself. He tried to cover his nakedness in the garden. Jesus did just the opposite. He uncovered Himself and became vulnerable to the disciples in order to wash their feet and be an example to us. He is raising up men for these times to be responsible to God. He is calling you by name.

❖   ✳   ❖

In a time when simple remarks such as "How's the family, still disintegrating?" bounce around in comedy clubs, the truth is alarming. Soaring statistics of family decline have caused some sociologists to proclaim the family an endangered species. Yet God created the family model. He gave us the choice to reverse the trend and live in obedience to His will. Man, getting right with His God, is not a denominational move nor is it a cultural one. It has nothing to do with gender. It is a move of God, and in that process, people will be drawn to Christ.

Reviewing the seven promises of a Promise Keeper, I came to recognize that the family is benefited in four areas:

- God is the Promise Maker.
- Men are the Promise Keepers.
- Women are the Promise Reapers.
- Children are the Promise Seekers.

It was the Lord who decided, "Let us make man." Therefore, everything that man is must be centered around what God had in His heart. God is the divine potter, and we are clay in His hands. We owe Him our absolute allegiance. It's a stunning truth: God made us in His image. Even though we are fallen creatures, He sees us not as we are but as He ordained us to be.

It surprises many that God chose to create the angels before creating man. This is fascinating because, like man, angels had nothing to say about their being created. It was solely in God's mind. They existed simply because God wanted them to, and yet what made them so significantly different was that, even in their creative order, they were given choices. When Satan led the high treason recorded in Isaiah 14 and Ezekiel 28, two-thirds of the angels chose to remain in heaven. The other third rebelled. Those who remained in heaven did so of their own volition, not because God decreed it. The environment of heaven changed from the initial creative order of the beginning. The position of the faithful angels' will was eternally sealed in the will of God.

Likewise, man was created by God. It was God's work and heart that made Adam. Confronted by temptation in the garden, Adam, like the angels, had a choice: to remain in the will of God or to violate the will of God. Adam was given three abilities that made him like God. He possessed the ability to choose, the ability to reason, and he was made in the image or character of God. With those three qualities, he could rule and reign in all of creation. When he yielded to temptation he violated the character of God (the will of God), and when he reasoned to eat the forbidden fruit from the tree of life, he fell out of fellowship with God.

Through the obedience of Jesus to His Father, a way was made for man to be restored. Good news for a man and his God!

> For if by the transgression of the one, death reigned through the one, much more those who receive the abundance of grace and of the gift of righteousness will reign in life through the One, Jesus Christ.
>
> *Romans* 5:17, NASB

Now when one is born again, he is no longer in the earth and the kingdom just because God wants him to be; he is there because he chose to be there and is therefore sealed in heaven! God decided to give each person a choice. Now, through our obedience, the will of God and the will of man come together. As surely as the angels who chose obedience over rebellion have their wills sealed in heaven, so, through your obedience, you are sealed, or hidden, with Christ in God. This is the foundation of faith.

Beyond the initial decision, after being born again, Hebrews 5 and 6 present the process of seeing what God will do in the life of a believer. Take the time to read these two chapters. God longs for each one to go on to maturity.

Therefore, leaving the discussion of the elementary principles of Christ, let us go on to perfection, not laying again the foundation of repentance from dead works and of faith toward God.

Hebrews 6:1

This is accomplished by the doctrine of perfection: being perfected into Christlikeness. We are changed by our intimacy with God. Prayer is God's call to bring us into His face. We are literally changed by the glory of "hangin' around with the Lord." One brother says, "We become who we hang around with." Prayer is hangin' around with God, and as we do we see God keeping His word. He watches over His word to perform it. That which is in the nature of God becomes our nature. What we see in God we deeply desire for ourselves. That leads us to be a man of the word. Conversely, God backs His word for it is His bond, and we are committed to backing our word. We are sealed in His integrity.

Early in Genesis, God said to Adam and Eve, "Be fruitful and multiply and replenish the earth." Most people think this is referring to having babies, but that is only half the story. When a man takes a wife, his children are not only the physical fruit of the marriage, but they become the first fruit of his lifestyle and character. When God told Adam and Eve to fill the earth, He was telling them to fill the earth with the character and image of Himself.

You Are Sowing Character into Your Children

You and I at this very time are sowing character into our children. This is called impartation. God will impart His image or character to us if we will let Him. Only then, as we are yielded over and become totally the fruit of who God is, can we pass this rich heritage of God down to our children.

It is easy to neglect the truth that marriage produces character fruit—not just biological fruit—from intimacy. Just as God declared, we will produce after our kind. Why should God allow us to get married and have children if we are going to produce a seed that is not like Him and will become His enemies? God's plan is that our children become the fruit of who we are, therefore reflecting God.

If we have ears to hear this truth it will strategically affect our mentoring others, starting with our children. Our first line of discipleship involves our very own children. We are to ask ourselves as men of God, "Is there anyone who wants to be like us?" Is there anyone you want to be mentored by and to be like? We are followers of men who by faith and patience inherit the promise. We have men who then follow us because we are heirs of that promise. Our highest aim is that our children—natural and spiritual—are like us in Christ and produce after our kind. This is why the apostle Paul could say with confidence and humility, "Follow my example."

We must ask ourselves, "Am I trying to develop or mentor by precept only?" Or by precept and practice? I am reminded of Elijah and Elisha. At the end of Elijah's life, Elisha would not leave his presence because he wanted the substance, the essence, the spirit of what the other had. Elijah literally passed down to Elisha the substance of his life.

We find this model true as God established the patriarchs Abraham, Isaac, and Jacob. I am the God of Abraham (one generation), Isaac (another generation), and Jacob (the third generation). These men not only passed down their natural inheritance, they passed down the essence of who they were: their spiritual inheritance and their character inheritance. Each had a personal encounter with God. They built on the fruit of their fathers and passed down what they received from God to their children. This is generational progression, and you and I are in the thick of it right now with our children and those who observe how we live our lives.

Pursuing vital relationships with the rare truth of God's plan prepares a man to mentor and be mentored in his own home and in the extended family of God. Truly, one generation to another should praise the Lord in an ever-growing throng from the seeds you are planting in the lives of those around you. Honoring Christ and building relationships, first in the home and then in the marketplace, are foundational to a man, his integrity, and God's plan to fill the earth.

In the Old Testament, on the headpiece of the high priest was written "Holiness Unto the Lord." One of the qualities of God's nature is that He is holy. God declares:

Be holy, for I am holy.

Leviticus 11:44

Many look at holiness as a bunch of rules. Believing that holiness is out of reach, the very idea gets dismissed. But the true believer has got to take personal holiness seriously. God demanded it, and it is the seed of the reality of God inside us. We are called to walk in holiness. Righteousness is the outward working of holiness, and in that context we walk in purity.

We Are No Greater Than We Are Pure

Christian men, we are no greater than we are pure. The most significant description a man can have said about him is that he is a man of God. He is righteous and honest.

In no way do we live in a gray-colored world. Our yeas are to be yeas and our nays should be nays. When Jesus becomes our standard, we do not commit sins of the body because it is no longer in our nature. There is no sex outside of marriage because we are determined not to break the covenant once we are married. Why does God hate divorce? Because He has established marriage as a physical manifestation of an invisible reality. Marriage models our relationship to Christ. Jesus married the church and will never divorce it. When we defy God and divorce we are mismodeling the church's relationship to Christ.

We learn to keep our word to our own hurt, even if we are not getting along in our relationships. When we become willing to be changed by constructive observations, we develop an awareness that opposites attract and likes often repel. Our differences may be used to make us one. In reality our purity is proof of our differences, not our agreements. We keep our covenants because we are men of integrity, not because we have to or are forced to by law, but because we want to. Jesus warns us to guard our hearts, our integrity, because out of them are the issues of life.

It is often said that an unguarded heart leads to disaster, but a well-guarded heart brings peace. Timothy reminds us to:

> guard through the Holy Spirit who dwells in us, the treasure which has been entrusted to you.
>
> *2 Timothy* 1:14

I really enjoy hearing about God's blessing of love in the life of a man and his family. As we look at the Genesis account, we again learn that it was God's idea to bring the woman to man. After this was accomplished, God looked at the two of them and said, "It is very good." What a goal, that every marriage should be ordained by God to be very good.

Marriage and home were designed to model the ultimate destiny we are headed toward, the marriage supper of the Lamb. It was the Lord Himself who performed the first ceremony. This is so interesting because God created woman for the man; however, He did not bring them together for each other, He brought them together for Himself!

Don't shout me down. These pages may appear radical to your understanding in the past. Stay with me as we look at God's pattern for families. When you married your wife, the most important thing to comprehend is that this is something God brought about. God ordained marriage. Not only in the earth, but before the foundation of the world He wanted you to be together. He confirmed in Genesis 2 that it was not good for man to be alone.

Most of us know the story of when God caused a deep sleep to come on Adam, and He took one of his ribs, or as Hebrew wisdom relates, "one of his sides." From this God made the woman and brought her to the man.

Amazingly, God had already set the vision for what was to be and she was brought to Adam so the two of them together could fulfill God's will. The idea that God brings two together to meet the other's need is how marriage is viewed and thought of today. On the contrary, God brings the two together to meet His need so that the whole home will be brought into the vision and purpose of God. There is a mandate when God says to the man, "take dominion." That dominion mandate is a corporate domination because God created man in His own image.

In the bosom of the man, the woman was there, and God spoke, even in creative order, knowing the two of them were created to fulfill His eternal plan. By prophetic proclamation the man relates, "This is now bone of my bones and flesh of my flesh; She shall be called Woman, because she was taken out of Man" (Gen. 2:23). She was called woman because she was literally taken from his flesh. It is important to remember that she came from his side, not from his feet to be walked on, nor his head to be ruled over, but from his side, the closest place next to his heart, to be embraced as the two become one.

Our calling in marriage is to model Christ's love for the church, therefore, a man's first line of responsibility is to be devoted to his wife.

> Therefore a man shall leave his father and mother and be joined to his wife, and they shall become one flesh.
>
> *Genesis 2:24*

At this time in creation, there were no mothers and fathers, and yet Adam was able to prophetically see into the future of the creative order. He was made perfect and therefore knew in advance the tensions of a home and spoke of the responsibilities of a man and his wife, who was to be his partner in ministry. It is important to notice that it is not just a man's ministry; it is a ministry for the whole home in the creative purposes of God. A man demonstrates to his wife, as God through Christ demonstrates to the church.

God set forth several things Adam was to do for his wife. He was to share with her God's vision for the home because man becomes the visionary in the home, declaring the will of the Lord for the family. He was to see to it that she was included. Without her, he is only half the man to fulfill the vision. He makes certain that she is joined to him, not as an appendage, but as a partner, joined by covenant in and to do the will of God. It is descriptive of when we marry and are sealed by covenant and that we are united with the Lord in purpose.

The Principle of Leadership Is Simple

Adam was to serve his wife and, in my opinion, outserve her! Yes sir! A lot of men wander around trying to be leaders in their home, believing that leading is making the family do what they themselves want. These types will always be frustrated. When they forge ahead with their plans and look over their shoulder, there is rarely anybody there. If anyone is following, it is usually out of fear and obligation, not love. But don't waste your time. Life is too short.

The principle of leadership is so simple. The Bible states, "He that is greatest among you, let him become as a servant." Do you want to lead in your home? Do you want to be honored and respected by your wife and family? Then lay awake at night trying to think of ways to outserve your wife. Christ took His cloak off to wash the disciples feet. You are instructed, Christian man, to love your wife as Christ loved the church. Remarkably, when a woman sees her husband outserving her, she tends to get pretty serious about not letting him get ahead of her. This divine competitiveness brings a harvest of love, honor, and respect. If you think you are going to be the leader in your home without being the greatest servant in your house, you are just making life tough on yourself.

Woman was to be blessed every day and prayed over. It is the man's responsibility to sow affirmation in his wife even as Jesus sees the church and blesses it in advance of any responsibility. Each man walking with God is to bless his wife, continually affirming her before the Lord, the family, and the world.

It is fascinating to look at the details presented in the Bible. Eve did not receive her name until after the Fall. This is significant because today we hear the preacher performing a marriage ceremony, representing God in the process of marriage, declaring when it is over," I now present to you, Mr. and Mrs. Wellington Boone." Eve was Mrs. Adam because they became one. Even as the church is called the body of Christ. They had no separate or hyphenated names. They were one.

As they were one in union so they were to be one in action. This relates to how their children were to be raised. I have often told my three children, "If you mess with my woman, you have my wrath!" They know I am serious because I back my wife's leadership in our home. Because I desire to make her happy, I will not allow my children to make her sad. They are part of my vision to bring her joy.

Children must be disciplined, and I believe the man is deeply involved in this aspect of the family. Our wives are not to do it all. Even from the birth of our offspring, the first voice each child heard belonged to their daddy. I declared the word of God in their lives. I set a standard. When they cried at night, I shared the responsibility of getting up and assuring them, "I am here. I am with you." I assisted with their homework and helped tuck them in bed at night. I wanted my voice to be familiar to them both as a symbol of authority and also great love.

The biblical model describes me as a man of God, a disciple under authority. I want my family to see that, as I disciple them, I am being discipled by God. The Bible asks, "If you do not know how to submit to another, how can God give you anything of your own?"

❖　＊　❖

Even as man is the promise keeper, so the wife is the promise reaper. The Bible precisely speaks to her: Submit to your husband as to the Lord (Col. 3:18). Initially she is called to submit, but also to go to a deeper level. In so doing she is submitting to the Lord. It is important to dispel any issues as to the level of submission. The definition and declaration of submission are as follows: The degree to which a wife submits to her husband is the degree to which she is submitted to God. A wife's level of submission to her husband is the physical manifestation of an invisible reality—her level of submission to God.

Certainly husbands are less than perfect, but the wife's submitting is not targeted to the husband but to the Perfect One. The subject goes still to a higher level. In 1 Peter 2 there is a discussion of what it means to be servants or slaves of God.

> Servants, be submissive to your masters with all fear, not only to the good and gentle, but also to the harsh.
>
> 1 Peter 2:18

The very suggestion of submission brings forth a series of what ifs. What if the husband is not saved? What if he does ungodly things? Such queries answer a myriad of questions because they reveal the attitude, and submission is an attitude. It is an act of the will. With one's intellect, volition, and affection, as we submit to God, so our very submission models Jesus' reflection of His Father. Even if one is suffering wrongly and endures, it is commendable.

> For what credit is it if, when you are beaten for your faults, you take it patiently? But when you do good and suffer, if you take it patiently, this is commendable before God. For to this you were called, because Christ also suffered for us, leaving us an example, that you should follow His steps.
>
> 1 Peter 2:20–21

Many sociologists define men and women as instrumental and expressive with the man being stronger physically. Women may tend to shrug off submissiveness, not by physical prowess, but with their tongues, using harsh, biting words. Submission disciplines the tongue. The Word says we are not to let guile be found in our mouths. Romans 4 and Proverbs 4 move to another level with the message that out of the heart are the issues of life, and Romans 10, with the mouth, confession is made unto salvation. Words do have meaning. Out of the abundance of the heart the mouth speaks.

Following in Jesus' steps offers a tough choice.

> Who committed no sin, nor was deceit found in His mouth; who, when He was reviled, did not revile in return; when He suffered, He did not threaten, but committed Himself to Him who judges righteously; who Himself bore our sins in His own body on the tree, that we, having died to sins, might live for righteousness; by whose stripes you were healed.
>
> 1 *Peter* 2:22–24

Many people misinterpret those lines, "by whose stripes you were healed," pointing toward physical healing. However, that is not the context. It relates to the healing of an inappropriate character. The atoning work of Jesus is how we are healed. It pictures sheep going astray, now returning to the shepherd, the bishop of our souls. First by death, then by His resurrected life, we are invited to follow His model.

God and His Word Are One

As we study God's Word, we continue to see Him as the explanation for everything and that He and His Word are one. Notice the details of Scripture. Revealing that He is "the bishop of our souls," relates to our emotion, our will, and our mind. He graciously becomes the One who answers the discomfort we may encounter as we follow His lifestyle.

There is real power in submission in marriage.

> Wives, likewise, be submissive to your own husbands, that even if some do not obey the word, they, without a word, may be won by the conduct of their wives.
>
> 1 *Peter* 3:1

Again, the church is Christ's bride, and with such an example, the wife models to the husband the visible manifestation of the church. A standard is set to slaves with unrighteous masters and to wives with unrighteous husbands. As slaves suffer wrongfully, so do wives, but neither miss God's attention.

One wife who had suffered abuse and pain was reading her Bible one day. She often asked where Jesus was when her husband mistreated her. Didn't God care? Then in quiet reflection she read that His compassion never fails. It spoke to her heart. Where was He when she was battered and broken? He was always there, even when she hurt so much she could not sense Him. This was the evidence she needed to reveal to her how intensely God cares for His own and their infirmities. He puts our tears into a bottle. He is touched by our grief. After thirty-four years of being a Christ-model to an unworthy husband, his hard heart was broken and he believed in her God.

There is another area of subjection that is interesting in the historical study of slavery. When a person is born again, there is a name change. When a person is married, there is a name change. In essence, one loses identity with previous family. The new identity is with the new family, the new destiny is the husband's destiny. The new name, Christian, denotes a servant to Jesus and a slave to God. If the Son sets you free, you are free indeed. Free to become a slave to God and to serve Him with joy and gladness.

The slave loses his identity to his master, even as a wife does to her husband. It is representative of the kingdom. For to the degree one loses his own identity and is immersed in the new identity is the degree to which one will reflect Christ. An example is given of the servant in Luke.

> And which of you, having a servant plowing or tending sheep, will say to him when he has come in from the field, "Come at once and sit down to eat?" But will he not rather say to him, "Prepare something for my supper, and gird yourself and serve me till I have eaten and drunk, and afterward you will eat and drink"?
>
> *Luke* 17:7–8

It strikes me that today when a man goes to work and comes home, the wife may be annoyed with his attitude to "make ready and serve." The model Jesus was teaching was a comparison with the church and the woman, again as the bride of Christ and her subjection to Christ.

In Far Eastern and Hebrew cultures where the Bible originated, this was and most often still is the case. That is what occurs with the church. It sits down last at the table, for the master is at the head and we are serving Him.

Notice this magnificent picture. It is something that God is building from within. He uses from the earth, the physical church, and, from the home, that visible manifestation of an invisible reality. Our attitudes, ways, and thoughts reveal how we are spiritually before God, and this gives the opportunity to witness likeness to the kingdom.

We Aren't Judged by Position but for Faithfulness in That Position

Does God thank the servant because he did what is commanded? Women are prone to want to ignore this passage. It becomes troublesome. However, we are partners in the marriage, with the husband being the head. In nature a two-headed animal is an anomaly. These responsibilities are differentiated by authority structures. The Bible never says who is better or who is less. I want to emphasize, the roles are divided. We must remember the truth of these teachings relates that one is not judged by position, but for faithfulness in that position whether you are the CEO of a corporation or a husband in the family. Eternally we are monitored for our attitude and how we handle the character of Christ in our calling. There are times when, in the context of salvation, the husband may be saved, but the wife will have more rewards because of more faithful service to the Lord. I know a lot of wives who wash their husbands clothes here on earth, but in heaven those husbands are going to be washing their wife's feet!

The issue is not value. The issue is roles and faithfulness in those roles. That is why God's judging will be absolutely fair. He is the one who decided who would be male, who would be female, and who would have position. Western thought presents the issue according to the authority structure to determine value. But God says that He does not give value for position. He values the manner in which you handle your position.

These concepts may bring much resistance today. In looking at our world, however, the Promise Keepers' commitment to building strong marriages and families through love, protection, and biblical values are not recommendations or suggestions from God. They are commands. Family harmony is a direct result of biblical harmony. God's commands carry the wonderful promise that He is with us—always.

Luke 17 continues these issues by stating, after the symbolic supper was served,

> Does he thank that servant because he did the things that were commanded him? I think not. So likewise you, when you have done all those things which you are commanded, say, "We are unprofitable servants. We have done what was our duty to do."
>
> *Luke* 17:9–10

It is all too common for many husbands to be ungrateful, to never pause to say thank you or to affirm their wife as she cooks, looks after the kids, keeps the house or holds down a job to help augment family finances. While this is difficult to accept, it can be sustained by looking to the Lord. His affirmation is the highest form of praise.

> How can you believe, who receive honor from one another, and do not seek the honor that comes from the only God?
>
> *John* 5:44

Romans relates that with honor we are to prefer one another, with the highest preference going to God. Approval should not be horizontal, but vertical, because receiving rewards in heaven and on this earth has nothing to do with gender. For when you have done all that is commanded, the reasonable service and duty have been accomplished and you have glorified God.

In reflecting on people who model Christ, I am reminded of Smith Wigglesworth, an evangelist and man of God years ago. He was traveling on a train and seated in the dining car.

While eating his dinner, a man came up to him and said, "You convicted me of sin. How can I get saved?" Why did this happen? The glory of God was so strong with this man that he brought people into the kingdom of God without opening his mouth. Such power is entrusted to a wife, with the supernatural approval of God through her, though she is suffering in the flesh.

First Peter records the importance of holding "chaste conduct, coupled with fear," speaking of reverence to the husband and is indicative of the church's reverence for Christ. The wife's role is further identified with the words to not:

> let your adornment be merely outward adorning . . . rather let it be the hidden person of the heart, with the incorruptible beauty of a gentle and quiet spirit, which is very precious in the sight of God.
>
> 1 Peter 3:3–4

Feminists scoff at these truths laid down before the foundation of the world. In their desperate struggle against being slaves, they have become lonely slaves to their own cause.

I find these truths incredible in teaching God-ordained roles for men and women. We have a tendency to put on attractiveness from the outside. Women put on to increase their outward appearance, to be beautiful. The Lord said that if you will walk like Him in submission, He would provide a different kind of lavish beauty—the magnificence of the beauty of holiness. Even as we put on coverings for the outside, God has invited us to allow Him to grow our beauty from within, specifically, the beauty of a meek and quiet spirit. Indeed, man does look on the outward appearance but God chooses to monitor the heart. J. B. Phillips said that such "meekness isn't weakness, but strength harnessed for service."

Modern-day women modeling the beauty of holiness are rare. Godly beauty is just like a magnet that draws individuals into the kingdom. A young girl asked me if Mrs. Adam would ever have been tempted to visit a cosmetic counter. She had the notion that Eve was perfect before the Fall but needed a face-lift afterward. Serious about becoming the woman God wanted her to be, she "saw" with her spiritual eyes that more influence was placed on outward appearance after the Fall. When it comes to such questions I have a simple answer. There is nothing wrong with makeup unless it hides you. This young woman made a commitment to be defined by what was on the inside. She placed on her makeup mirror, "The beauty of holiness unto the Lord."

Following a Promise Keepers appearance in Detroit, my church service was visited four times by a pastor in his early forties. He related that, in retrospect, he had so much information presented to him in those four sessions that he felt lost and confused. He suggested I take it slower.

Mulling over the emphasis on creative order, roles, and relationships, he wondered if this teaching was too radical for the present day. In a way he was right. God's teaching will become more and more radical as we get further from His plan. What this pastor was really discovering was that his personal life was not in order. He and his wife were like two ships passing in the night. Their children were being parented more by church members than by them. He also had a hidden desire for pornographic videos. He used them to help him "relax."

Driven by seed sown from the Word, he moved back to the Genesis account I continually presented. He confronted head-on how out of step his family was with God's plan, and, more alarming, how co-dependent his church was on his erring ways. Through the Word, piercing like a two-edged sword, he began the "trip back to where it began, in the Garden of Eden, and my wife and children and I started over, not my way, but God's way." Stunned by the sudden conviction that moved across his church and people, and seeing his model as a pastor, he is moving forward "strictly, willingly, and studying to prepare for being part of God's forever family."

Sadly, the first half of this story is not unusual. Christians have become safe, comfortable, and often complacent, truly at ease in Zion. God wants to do a new thing. It takes serious effort to move ahead God's way, as the dramatically changed pastor said. Being willing to be conformed to His image is painful, discouraging, often misunderstood, but always transforming. In the process, heaven rejoices!

He saw with the eyes of his limited understanding the parallel relationship of husband and wife, wife and church. "Husbands, love your wives, just as Christ also loved the church and gave Himself for her" (Eph. 5:25). The church is to be sanctified, cleansed, and presented as glorious, without spot or wrinkle. Literally, holy, without blemish. How could a church be pure when the pastor was impure and imitated the world more than the Lord?

This is the real vision God has for the church. It becomes an instrument that He Himself compares to marriage. He lays down a template of the husband as the example to his wife of what the church invisible—as the bride of Christ—looks like. Bringing this into today, the question is asked, "What is the Lord doing now for the church?"

He is cleansing it and getting it ready for a great marriage. We, as His children, are to be about our Father's business, preparing our homes to be like His church. Our churches should be in line with Him. The Lord created man in His image and likeness. In creating woman to be with man, her reflection in the man is expressed as to where creation was headed. Ultimately we now know that Christ is going to marry a bride. What should that preparation resemble?

The man expresses unconditional love to his wife. The pastor becomes the model of expressing unconditional love toward his flock. This occurs because pastors raise up spiritual children preparing to be married to the Lord Jesus. The pastor is the under shepherd. He desires that his spiritual children, out of intimacy with the Holy Spirit, follow after his kind. They are his sheep. He cares for them, looks after them, is an example to them in his home and pulpit, and willingly sacrifices for them. He feeds them the Word and the substance of what they are to become. He prophesies to them their destiny. He leads them to the face of the Lord through his prayer life and is an example of the believer. His example draws others to want the same relationship with God, where your maker is your husband,

> The LORD of hosts is His name; And your Redeemer is the Holy One of Israel; He is called the God of the whole earth.
>
> *Isaiah 54:5*

The church becomes the woman who is being prepared as the bride of Christ. The sheep see this by looking at their pastor, into his home, and at his children. Then having become part of the sheepfold of his environment, his flock can look at him, listen to him, and follow him as he follows Christ.

Jesus is called the great shepherd of the sheep. A biblical example of this is found in Paul. He was an apostle and a pastor. He went into cities, seeing those who were lost and giving them the gospel. Those responding became his own. He exemplified Jesus. To the church of Corinth he wrote about changed lives that were fruit from his ministry.

> You are our epistle written in our hearts, known and read by all men; clearly you are an epistle of Christ, ministered

by us, written not with ink but by the Spirit of the living God, not on tablets of stone but on tablets of flesh, that is, of the heart.

2 Corinthians 3:2–3

He was reminding the church that when people see his sheep, they know who the father is because they take on the attributes of their father.

A father took his young daughter to visit a blind shut-in. The woman had only been blind for six years. She knew the father well. When the five-year-old was introduced to the blind woman, she took the youngster's face in her hands and felt every detail of her face and expression. When the child drew back, her simple statement was, "Please understand, I am examining you for evidences of your father."

So our heavenly Father examines us for how we reveal and reflect Him. A pastor's sheep will take on the persona of the pastor. The church becomes a family. In Ephesians 3, the whole family of God is named, and as that family takes on the name of God as Father, together they build the kingdom.

It is interesting that Paul, in discussing the mystery of the church, shares his concerns and encouragement.

Therefore I ask that you do not lose heart at my tribulations for you, which is your glory. For this reason I bow my knees to the Father of our Lord Jesus Christ, from whom the whole family in heaven and earth is named, that He would grant you, according to the riches of His glory, to be strengthened with might through His Spirit in the inner man, that Christ may dwell in your hearts through faith; that you, being rooted and grounded in love, may be able to comprehend with all the saints what is the width and length and depth and height—to know the love of Christ which passes knowledge; that you may be filled with all the fullness of God.

Ephesians 3:13–19

He was raising up spiritual children, preparing them to be with the Lord. We are learning to become part of the faithful family of the Lord. We have identity with God as our Father and are heirs of the inheritance.

Hebrew teaching prepares the eldest son in each family to be prepared when he comes of age. At that time, the father is ready to die. The father is to bring up the elder son for receiving the inheritance. Likewise, this is the goal of the shepherd of the sheep, to bring his people to maturity so that they might assume the responsibility of the shepherd. Modeled by the words of Paul,

And He Himself gave some to be apostles, some prophets, some evangelists, and some pastors and teachers, for the equipping of the saints for the work of ministry, for the edifying of the body of Christ.

Ephesians 4:11–12

This explains that the saints, being prepared, are getting, not only precept, but practice in developing into the fivefold ministry. They were and are edifying in love.

The church is to be known by unconditional love. It is to be a family, people who come to be blessed. In the house of God compassion reigns, and when mistakes are made the first place a person should run for safety is to the church. In the church, one does not have to be innocent before receiving forgiveness. You receive forgiveness because you are guilty. The church is a place of acceptance, love, and preparation for overcoming.

Therefore, leaving the discussion of the elementary principles of Christ, let us go on to perfection, not laying
again the foundation of repentance from dead works and
of faith toward God, of the doctrine of baptisms, of laying
on of hands, of resurrection of the dead, and of eternal
judgment.

Hebrews 6:1–2

These principles lead us to maturity! No longer are we to be
content to be just receivers of truth, but teachers of the substance gained from the shepherd.

God's house is called a house of prayer. People come to His
house to have their needs met. It is a hospital where people
can be prayed for, spiritually, physically, and emotionally. From
such experiences, the church becomes the sent one to take
salt and light into an anxious society, desperately in need of
God's love and wholeness. It is the true family of God.

The Bible tells us that we must pray for those in authority
over us. To many, this suggests prayer for those in government.
The first prayer, because of the first line of authority, however, is
for the kingdom of God. The Hebrews recognized this, knowing
that the government of God is holy. The Levitical order outlined
the authority structure. As believers, we have gotten side-
tracked and out of step, so we put the secular ahead of sacred
authority. In the kingdom, authority comes from those who are
spiritual, those who are entrusted with the care of our souls.
Everything in the earth comes from that which is in the spirit.

We Are to Pray for Our Spiritual Leaders

One of my griefs is when I learn of a servant-shepherd who
wants to quit the ministry. These dear brothers are in good

company. Even Moses wanted to quit, having tired of dealing with the rebellious children of Israel.

> Then Moses heard the people weeping throughout their families, everyone at the door of his tent; and the anger of the LORD was greatly aroused; Moses also was displeased. So Moses said to the LORD, "Why have You afflicted Your servant? And why have I not found favor in Your sight, that You have laid the burden of all these people on me? Did I conceive all these people? Did I beget them, that You should say to me, 'Carry them in your bosom, as a guardian carries a nursing child,' to the land which You swore to their fathers? . . . I am not able to bear all these people alone, because the burden is too heavy for me. If You treat me like this, please kill me here and now; if I have found favor in Your sight; and do not let me see my wretchedness!"
>
> *Numbers* 11:10–12, 14–15

The anger of the Lord was evident. Moses, the shepherd of Israel, was displeased and asked why he had not found favor in God's sight. He was so heavily burdened by the people, he preferred death to life because of the burden those Israelites had placed upon him.

He was not saying, "If you make things better, God, keep me alive or give me the strength to endure." He was so overcome by the striving he was ready to lay down and die.

Do You Make Your Pastor Want to Quit the Ministry?

I ask you, Do you make your pastor want to quit the ministry? Are you such a burden to him and do you put so much pressure on him that he's ready to give up? Is it possible you see him as a spiritual Santa Claus rather than your shepherd? God wants you to serve Him with your feet, not just your hands. He wants you to model Christ with your lifestyle so you can join your pastor in the work of the ministry and not just show up on Sunday for what you can get.

You should be a source of supply to your pastor. Every dad wants his children to come to the place where they make him proud. What does he expect? When he feeds you, you receive and consistently grow in maturity and prove yourself faithful. The Bible says it is required of a steward to be faithful. When the pastor's people take responsibility, feed on the Word, and can be counted on in any situation, it is doubtful his resignation is imminent.

When I was in Nashville with several country western musicians who were visible artists, I asked them if they could be counted on in their churches now that they had risen to stardom. Could their pastor depend on them? Were they churchgoers or part of the church that is going? Do they faithfully tithe? Many identified with me when I shared how easy it is to tithe when one's income is moderate. But when the bank balances soar and the certificates of deposit stack high, could they still be counted on? Did they attend services on Wednesday nights? Were they faithful choir members when in town, or did they feel excused because music was their profession?

Many as they climb are not willing to take on the task of being a doorkeeper in the house of God. Such a station is too low. We count on our pastors, but can they count on us? The Lord wants to change you. He, like every father, when it comes to crunch time, desires His children to be faithful, available, and teachable.

We Count on Our Pastors
but Can They Count on Us?

Promise Keepers are called to be faithful in the house of God. They need to continue moving into higher levels of commitment.

What a great challenge in front of us to reach out across denominational and racial lines. To not look through ethnic or colored glasses on the issues of life, but be willing to confront the injustices of the past with the reconciliation of God's love. Jesus' high priestly prayer is for all believers.

> I do not pray for these alone, but also for those who will believe in Me through their word; that they all may be one, as You, Father, are in Me, and I in You; that they also may be one in Us, that the world may believe that You sent Me.
>
> John 17:20–21

He clearly states that we are one with one another and one with Him, united in mind, will, and the ways of the Father. His desire is that we be one with Him as He is with His Father. Being united as one, the world will see and know we are disciples because of our love for one another.

True Christians are beyond natural explanation when the world observes our unity. The harmony stems from being a true disciple of Christ. The world cannot find a like model. We ought to be so glorious in our relationships with one another that it is attractive and puzzling to those around us. We should naturally create a loving environment with no barriers.

If Adam had not sinned, we would no doubt all be kin, but his sinning seed brought death. If he had been obedient to God, he would be alive and we would all be brothers.

In Christ, as Christians, we are brothers and sisters. Why? If God is your father, then I am your brother. We are family! Christ is our brother, God is our father, and in response to that, I quote the country people of Tennessee and North Carolina, "We are kin folk!" True Christians even share similar family characteristics, called the fruit of the spirit. No matter our color, we resemble one another because we have the same Father. We all have different personalities, but we share the qualities of the One who created us; qualities such as love, joy, peace, long-suffering, kindness, goodness, faithfulness, gentleness, and self-control. It should come as no surprise that it is written of this family of God that by their fruit you will know them.

It is obvious we all have faults, but we are being developed, becoming now what we already are in Christ. All the fruit of our lives evolves from love, the greatest of all gifts. How we get along with our brothers, handle situations, and reach out to treat all people as God would treat them reflects who we are. In these areas, we find God literally a God of breaking through.

God has not just recently called us to unity in Christ, we are already unified. I am surprised that many are rushing to the year 2000 with concepts of unification. Unify 2000 and other organizations point toward the century's turn. When I talk about Unified 2000, I am talking about old news—what took place two thousand years ago. That is when Jesus was raised from the dead and when He declared, "We are one." If we are not one as brothers today, we are two thousand years behind the finished work of Christ. The only issue is not disunity; the issue is our carnality. Paul spoke to this when he told his church:

And I, brethren, could not speak to you as to spiritual people but as to carnal, as to babes in Christ.

1 *Corinthians* 3:1

He chided the church when he described them as carnal and walking as men, not committed followers of God. He dealt with people who were divided, not because the people were racist, but because they were carnal. The issue of racial division is an issue of spiritual immaturity and carnality. Get rid of the carnality and maturity will dominate over the problems in the church of Jesus Christ.

The Lord Didn't Wait Until After We Were Changed . . . He Sent His Son to Bring Change

All races are our brothers and sisters. As a result I can stand up and look in the face of so-called rednecks and say they are loved in my church. Why? Because the Lord did not wait until after we had changed to send His Son. He sent His Son to bring change. We have to love in advance of affirmative action. In that regard, we reach out and demonstrate unconditional love. It is called agape love, the kind that shows off under pressure. It is not moved by the actions or inaction of a person; it is an innate part of your nature. Because love is as strong as death, the love in me will defeat the hatred in you.

Agape Love Shows Off Under Pressure

One particular brother—from a family of rednecks—but an outstanding young man himself, said to me, "You are more of a father to me than my own father." His father was a member of the Ku Klux Klan. Crosses were burned on the land of my former church. This young man hugged me. We were one. Even though my skin is chocolate, my spirit is white because it follows after righteousness, and that is the color that we all are in Christ. White is clean and pure as He is because of what He accomplished for us all on the cross. Not white as in race, but white as in grace, because the glory and goodness of God has come upon us through His shed blood. He has been merciful to us. So we are mandated to not only love our brother, but to demonstrate that love. Love has a lot of work to do! I'm here to tell you that I love those high-truck ridin', Seven-Eleven stoppin', tobacco-chewin', spittin', Confederate-flag-totin' brothers!

Let me ask you some questions. What color is love? What gender is kindness? What socioeconomic level is gentleness? Do you want to fellowship with your own kind? Then open your arms and heart to all the people of God. No matter what they look, sound, smell, walk, or talk like—they're your brothers.

If You Don't Like People Who Are Different You Won't Fit into Heaven

As a black, it was not sufficient for me to forgive the white community lightly. Forgiveness came because the love of Christ constrained me to reach out and embrace them as mine and to walk with them in the character of Christ. If I show favoritism or preferences because of my culture to be around other blacks or if I talk condescendingly about whites when they are not around, then I am guilty of causing disunity in the body of Christ. I become hypocritical because God is no respecter of persons. His cross-shaped heart displays a wide-open invitation that "whosoever will may come." I mismodel the kingdom if I show one thing on the outside of my life and the inside speaks something different.

That is exactly how the devil works. He masquerades as an angel of light. He puts on the right cover, but inside, like Jesus said to the Pharisees, "You are a white-washed tombstone." White on the outside but inside, total death and darkness. We must remove that darkness from us!

As white people reach out to blacks and blacks to whites, we become a unified, holy nation, a royal priesthood in the family of God. This is magnificently illustrated in Revelation.

After these things I looked, and behold, a great multitude which no one could number, of all nations, tribes, peoples, and tongues, standing before the throne and before the Lamb, clothed with white robes, with palm branches in their hands, and crying out with a loud voice, saying, "Salvation belongs to our God."

Revelation 7:9–10

If I envision heaven with all its races and languages, and God's will is done on earth as in heaven, then I have to envision the same in my neighborhood, city, and world. If I am racist and cannot accept someone of another color whom God calls my brother, then I can't be a Christian. Jesus said you cannot love Me and hate your brother. If you don't open your heart to the unity of Christ you won't fit into heaven when the time comes. Jesus Christ declares that the people of heaven come from every tribe, people, and nation. If you harbor such feelings, you need to reevaluate your salvation. God expects more than heartless confession. He wants fruit that displays our confession in credibility and action. The flavor of the fruit is determined by its connection to the vine!

Under His authority, we are preparing to be stewards over the whole earth. With stewardship comes responsibility to bring others in this family. Christ has already paid the price for those outside His fold. We are challenged to move with a holy zeal, commissioned by God as His ambassadors.

Now then, we are ambassadors for Christ, as though God were pleading through us: we implore you on Christ's behalf, be reconciled to God.

2 Corinthians 5:20

As the waiting Father, He allows us to invite whosoever will to become part of His family. We are privileged to preach the word of grace and the absolute truth that He died and rose again. We are His representatives to speak words of deliverance to the world and to bring people to Christ. We are exporters of vision to the lost, having been granted the ministry of reconciliation and speaking words of reconciliation. In so doing we become attractive to the world and can lead them to a saving knowledge of Jesus Christ.

We are partakers of the greatest power ever known. Power to be used for the purposes of God in a prepared people. Thus we possess a world-view because we are seated with Him in heavenly places and can see through His eyes into the distances of God from His vantage point.

I recall teaching my daughter how to view "from the large to the small." I started by asking her what is the most important thing needed when putting together a puzzle? Being very bright, she responded, "I have to see the whole picture."

This is significant because if we try to interpret as a culture, such as a black person or a white person, we are on the level of the earth and cannot see far enough nor can our view encompass enough to see with kingdom vision.

From that vantage point, or the point from which we view, as the brothers say, the question becomes relevant. Where are you coming from? From the perspective of earth or heaven? Heaven encompasses being seated with Him, and from that perspective we can see all people with Jesus' eyes as one church. That is the view Christ imparts to His own.

Will you embrace God's vision for your life, your marriage, your family, and your world? God is calling you by name.

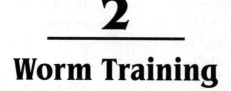

2

Worm Training

My God, my God, why hast thou forsaken me? Why art thou so far from helping me, and from the words of my roaring? . . . But I am a worm, and no man; a reproach of men, and despised of the people.

Psalm 22:1, 6, KJV

If you were to get a group of people together to talk about their dreams, it would be a far-ranging discussion. Our aspirations know few boundaries. Our desires take us to lofty places. One thing would be sure, no one in the group would admit to the hope of some day being like a worm. We never think about going down, only up.

While reading Scripture one day, I settled into Psalm 22, a messianic psalm. When Jesus hung on the cross, He cried out the same words found in this Psalm: "My God, my God, why has thou forsaken me?" A few verses later these words appear, "But I am a worm and I am no man." It struck me like a brick between the eyes. Instantly I understood the difference between rising up to defend one's self and the beauty of being crushed and broken before God.

Suddenly it was all clear. This is the problem in troubled marriages. This is what causes division among brothers, cultures, and nations. They have not yet learned how to become broken. We are so concerned about being taken advantage of that we miss the divine ministry to which we have been called.

How many times have we missed a divine appointment because nobody was going to step on us? Praise God that Jesus wasn't concerned about being taken advantage of!

We are called to be worms. When you step on a worm, what happens? You don't hear a sound. Not a peep of protest. It is crushed and that is the end of it. Isaiah 53:7 declared that Jesus would go to the cross like a lamb to the slaughter. He would go in silence, without protest. So He did. A worm never protests. A worm doesn't fight back. A worm doesn't find ways to escape a crushing blow from above. Can you say, for Christ, "I am a worm and am no man"? As common as worms are in the dirt, they are as rare and precious as fine diamonds in the church.

Unfortunately, there is another creature that more commonly represents our reaction to circumstances we don't like. The snake is the opposite of the worm. If you surprise a snake, he strikes. If you challenge a snake, he strikes. If you step on a snake, he strikes. A snake is into defending itself. Self-preservation is its number-one goal. Step on a snake, and it will writhe and twist and strike until it has killed or injured its assailant enough to get away.

How like snakes we are when we strike back as someone tries to get the better of us. Jesus said, "If anyone wants to sue you, and take your shirt, let him have your coat also" (Matt. 5:40, NASB). How similar to snakes we are when we are determined to maintain our position. Jesus said, "and whoever shall force you to go one mile, go with him two" (Matt. 5:41, NASB). How unlike worms we are when we are on our way to our divinely appointed slaughter and, instead of quietly focusing on the fact that nothing can separate us from the love of God, we writhe and strike back the entire way.

As a Christian you are in the power position. This is why it is so critical that, being a follower of Jesus Christ, you understand what occurred when Jesus washed the disciples' feet. Let's take another look at it.

> Jesus, knowing that the Father had given all things into His hands, and that He had come from God and was going to God, rose from supper and laid aside His garments, took a towel and girded Himself. After that, He poured water into a basin and began to wash the disciples' feet, and to wipe them with the towel with which He was girded.
>
> *John 13:3–5*

Our Lord proceeded knowing that God had given Him all things. It was from a position of great power and strength that He was motivated to take on the role of a servant. Being a worm requires the power of God because to achieve worm "status" you have to give up the world's standard of strength and position. This is impossible in the flesh. In our flesh we are all snakes, just waiting to strike.

We talked earlier about washing feet, but we need to reflect on this matter a little more deeply. I told you about the experience of washing the feet of one of God's great saints. I was incredibly privileged to be part of such a beautiful moment. But let's think for a moment what Jesus actually did. The Bible reveals that the disciples had already had supper by the time Jesus washed their feet. Apparently there was no servant to wash their feet when they came into the house as was customary, so, instead of washing each other's feet or even washing their own feet, they went to the table unwashed.

Jesus wasn't washing the feet of beautiful saints as I had the privilege to do. From a worldly standpoint they were a selfish, self-centered bunch who would not stand by Him in His hour of need. Yet, when He was finished, what did He say about what He had just done?

Do you know what I have done? . . . I have given you an
example, that you should do as I have done to you. . . .
If you know these things, blessed are you if you do them.

John 13:13–17

Did the disciples deserve to have their feet washed by the
Messiah? No. Were the disciples supersaints? No, not yet.
Jesus was acting toward His disciples as God acts toward us
and as we are expected to act toward others. Jesus saw His disciples for what God had ordained them to be, not what they
presently were. This is the perspective of a true worm, and it
can only come from a position of Godly power. From a human
standpoint there wasn't a reason in the world that the disciples should have their feet washed by Jesus. In fact, Peter per-
fectly represents the worldly view. There was no way he was
comfortable with Jesus' washing his feet. But Jesus knows who
we really are in God better than we know ourselves. He knows
that, as God's dear children, we contain within ourselves the
beautiful fragrance of the indwelling Holy Spirit. But if we are
never broken, like the bottle of costly perfume, that beautiful
fragrance will never fill a room in worship of Christ.

As you consider your brothers and sisters in the church
where you attend, are there any people there that are undeserving of your service? When you think of the ugly and selfish
impulses of people, do any names come to mind? How long is
your "unlovable" list? Those are the people whom God is asking you to see as He sees them. These are the people whose
feet Jesus made an example of—the very feet He wants you to
wash. If you find yourself unwilling to wash these feet, just
remember that you have lifted yourself up to the low status of
the unwashed disciples.

The black community particularly has failed to put their history into this context. When Jesus, as a worm, cried to His

Father, He was not answered. At the defining moment of His obedience, God closed His ears to His only son. Previously He had said, "My God always hears me." This time, God, in turning His back, elicited the gut-wrenching words, "But I am a worm, and I am no man."

Jesus was crushed like a worm. He was slapped. They spat in His face until it ran down his cheeks. A crown of thorns was pressed into his scalp, and ultimately he was abandoned by His disciples. At the point He needed them most, He was forsaken. He was so broken and weak that Simon of Niger had to carry His cross to Golgotha. But what did Jesus do? He went even further down. He knew the word.

> unless a grain of wheat falls into the ground and dies, it remains alone; but if it dies, it produces much grain.
>
> *John 12:24*

He gave in and became a worm. There is never a doubt that He possessed the power to raise Himself. Instead, He submitted to the point of death and yielded to the purposes of His Father. In turn, God raised Him up. God doesn't raise anything that is not dead.

God Doesn't Raise Anything That Is Not Dead

I will often repeat the message on my heart because I believe we learn from repetition and focusing our attention. I look out to the black community and call them to look at their condition and move past slavery. They have been badly treated, but I must remind them to not look at the past horizontally as people tend to do, but instead, look at it vertically, because God has never lost control of His people. Their past has a future. It is acquiring qualification to serve God. Those who have been slaves understand better than anyone the service to which Jesus has called His true disciples.

It is common to hear that people are out of control, but it will never be said that God is out of control. When we refuse to be a worm and be crushed for God, then we are out of control. Nothing escapes His mind. If you feel you have been off of His agenda for a time, never fear. The eyes of the Lord run to and fro throughout the earth. Nothing misses His view from the top.

If we allow God, like Jesus, to work into us the idea of worm training, it would be revolutionary. We'd gain a worm's eye view of what God wants to teach us about His business—kingdom business.

Taking on the form of a worm? Whoa, you say. That's a bit too much. But look at Christ. Are you falling? Keep your eyes on Him all the way down. What is the issue? Again, it is power. If God gives us power, and we still have revenge and personal agendas in our hearts, we will use that power selfishly and misappropriate it. God only gives power to servant-leaders, not power-hungry children.

Qualifying for leadership takes you only one direction. Down. God will raise those who have humbled themselves in His time and in His way. But first we have to become a servant, a worm, a bridge. If God is going to use you to be a bridge between estranged brothers and sisters, or between estranged cultures, then there is something about bridges you have to understand. Bridges, if they are to be used effectively to span the chasm, are to be walked on. "Therefore, holy brethren, partakers of the heavenly calling, consider the Apostle and High Priest of our confession, Christ Jesus, who was faithful to Him who appointed Him" (Heb. 3:1–2). An apostle is a sent one. In John 20:21 we have the statement, "Peace to you! As the Father has sent Me, I also send you." Jesus has become the evidence, the proof positive of the "sent one." Consider Him as the high priest of our confession. He became the great suspension bridge builder, from God to man. He honored His Father and exemplified the lifestyle we should follow. He was walked on. If you are going to be used of God, you too will be walked on.

If You Are Going to Be a Bridge for God, You Will Be Walked On

Think of the honor of being a bridge for and to God. Being willing to be walked on and walked over to take man to the Father. We need to submit our shoulders to Jesus, to become the foundation to hold up those who are in need. God wants to hold up His children as examples to the world. "Look! My followers are faithful. They bear my imprints all over their lives. Look how much they love me!" God desires our love and attention. We ask for so much and give Him so little.

I believe that in these final times on planet Earth we must inventory ourselves and discern just the way Jesus looks at us. He has the power to stop every mistreatment we receive just as He possessed the power to avoid death on the cross. We know this is not His way. Why? Because we are being trained to be His servants, slaves of God. As worms, we do not fight back. God is available twenty-four hours a day to hear the cry of those seeking Him.

A young girl came into a women's shelter at a rescue mission in Northern California. Her father was in prison. She had lived in foster homes and had given birth to a mixed-race baby at the age of fourteen. She remembered, with sadness, that she had been an honor student in junior high school. She hated her stepfather and had run away in rebellion. Moving from city to city, she found herself on skid row, stalked by a man who fed her a string of broken promises. She turned to cocaine. Her addiction led to prostitution. In desperation, she made every effort to escape its grip.

Like a revolving door, she went in and out of the mission. Often she would ask the leadership and counselors where God was when she was abused. Where was He when her father raped her and a series of men abused her as a child? Where was God when she was shot full of drugs and forced to sit in cheap bars and unsavory places?

One day while reading the Bible she came across two words that changed her life. "Jesus wept." Suddenly she felt the warmth and compassion of Father God, the great suspension bridge, who, through the cross, made provision for her to cross over into a new life. She realized "Jesus wept" during her torment. Wept for her and those who degraded her.

She is representative of thousands of girls who many count as disposable. To their pimps these teenage prostitutes are sequined, sedated gold mines. She discovered through the heart of Jesus what God could do with ruined things. Wrongly, she had been trained to be a slave to sinful men; now she has become a willing slave to God. As improbably and terrifying as her life has been, today she walks those same streets wearing a worm training cap on her blonde head, symbolizing being made low to rise again to usefulness in God's reclamation business. Reclaiming other young girls by hand and heart is her driving passion—all in the name of Jesus!

Wherever you are, God will take your brokenness and make something beautiful. Will you be a worm for God?

No Nation Is Stronger Than Its Weakest Link

My heart breaks for the cities of this world. Cities that keep girls of all ages in bondage. Cities that trick young children into a lifestyle of drug addiction. Cities that celebrate everything that is base and vile in this world. Startling statistics record that in the next few years there will be more than three hundred cities with a population of a million or more. This explosion of people ushers in a major influx of need. I think of and pray for our inner cities. They must be offered spiritual food so irresistible that they will partake even if they are unaware of being hungry. God's all-encompassing presence through His devoted "worms" must be a bridge over their troubled waters.

If White America Sneezes, Black America Catches a Cold

It is said that when white America sneezes, black America catches a cold. It is also true that if revival—worm revival— truly falls on the white community and focuses on the black community, revolution will result. God desires that His committed servants not abandon the inner city. We are to take His light to the darkest heart. You and I are given an opportunity to leave an imprint on this whole generation. Begin by being faithful where you are.

Statistics reveal that in 1959, 70 percent of black households had two parents. Ever since then those same figures have taken a toboggan slide downward. Two-parent homes are rare. One report indicated that as many as three-fourths of black households are single-parented, and the majority of those are women. The parallel between the disintegration of the black family and the emphasis on civil rights and government handouts is undeniable.

What really hurts me is that in the 1960s and even into the 1970s there was an outpouring of the Lord. God was granting our inalienable rights. Surprised? Those are rights given to us by God. What did God promise us? An outpouring of the Holy Spirit. What hasn't the black community in America had in almost a hundred years? An outpouring of the Holy Spirit. So while God was marching in places like Asbury College in 1970, pouring out His spirit, closing down the classrooms while students confessed sin and were getting saved, the black community marched toward the White House. They looked to man for a handout, whereas God was saying, "I want you to come to My altar. I want your total surrender, not your surrender to man's programs."

What was the outcome? The black community claimed its civil rights and scores in the white community received inalienable rights. The result is apparent today because blacks now exist in a vacuum larger than the one they had in the late 1950s and 1960s.

My cry is, God, will You not revive us again that Your people might rejoice in You? Through prayer and fasting my heartfelt plea is, God, save us now. I don't want to wait until the next generation for what You have ordained for this one. I am asking people everywhere to join me in seeking God to stem the incoming tide of sin that is threatening to bury this generation. There have never been more opportunities to share the love of Christ in the inner cities of this nation. Existing ministries need your support today. Your love will bring change.

I plead with the black community, don't let the march for handouts or black "inferiority" sweepstakes threaten to crowd out God's plan. Prevent the politicians from inflaming and then subjugating the people. Let's carry high His torch and light the revival fires with our love and concern. And, yes, our money. Let's not raise our hands for a government handout, but raise our hands in praise to almighty God the provider!

Remember in the days of Israel, God heard His children's cries because they were not addressing their pleas to the Pharaoh, but were beseeching God. We need to spread the message that God is the God of the underdog—what people wrongly perceive as the permanent underclass. He wants to lift high the cross and tell those snake oil politicians and preachers that there is no such entity as an underclass.

In Virginia, where we lived for years, the word "underclass" is a social designation for the lower classes. This designation is really a method of character assassination. The Bible in Isaiah 45 calls people who are in darkness "hidden treasures of darkness." God does not see us where we are. He sees us where He ordained us to be. Therefore, we call that which is not as though it is.

I am convinced the inner cities are waiting for people to give them a new vision because of their hunger for hope. A hunger that has yet to be satisfied. A friend of mine emphasizes Romans where it says where sin abounds, grace much more abounds. Kenneth Weiss says, "Where sin is in abundance, grace is in super abundance, and then some more on top of that!" Those trapped in the ghettos and housing projects will respond to words of a new destiny. It will be a frightful harvest if the voice offering that hope is not compelled by the love of Christ.

Before the 1960s some blacks in Louisiana were told that *poor* had nothing to do with empty pockets, *poor* was having poverty in your mind. Jesus offers to let this mind be in you that is also in Christ. The mind of Christ opens the door to being a recipient of ultimate truth and understanding. With the mind of Christ, even those at the lowest level will rise to their destiny. It has nothing to do with skin color. That is why I am so convinced that whites can bring revival to blacks in America because it is not bringing culture, it is bringing them the kingdom. The vacuum is one that only Jesus can fill, so every white person who has Jesus can realistically take Him to the inner cities. They are just waiting for the anointed. Cultural vision is tunnel vision. God makes the difference, not culture.

Kingdom vision rises above the historical sin of slavery. Sadly, blacks hate the very thing that gives them an advantage in God's economy.

Please understand me and let me underline and emphasize that slavery was and is wrong. Wrong because it was not ordained by God. God never planned for this nation to be a melting pot with one race singled out to be excluded. He ordained it to be a stewpot. Why? What does He say? "Thy will be done on earth as it is in heaven." Heaven will be a montage of people of all races, kindred, and tongues joining around the throne to worship the King and sing worthy is the Lamb that was slain.

The Lord wants us to go and take the cities. There is no better place to practice wormhood. Take whatever He has given you and that is what will transcend culture. Start with giving those you meet a blessing! Move ahead by seeing them with the eyes of Jesus. Then speak to them in love and compassion, not belittling, but fill them with the living words of life.

When Uganda gained its independence from Britain, the English looked back and said, "You will never make it without us." They left, giving them not a blessing but a negative statement, a curse. God is just the opposite of us. We wait for people to measure up before we give our blessing. God, through Jesus Christ, gives a blessing at the beginning. He views us as what we were ordained to be, not as we are. This is what Jesus did by washing the unworthy disciple's feet. We eulogize people when they die. Jesus eulogizes people as a send-off into an abundant life with Him.

Successful worm training requires an attitude of faith and commitment to Christ to get through the tough assignments. Faith comes by hearing, and hearing by the Word of God. The Lord will make the Bible real and vital to your life. But you must know the Word. I challenge people, young and old, to be people of the Word. Let His words displace yours, and God will fill you with power to reach the lost.

In our church and associations we call ourselves elders. The meaning is father, bishop, or overseer. Yet I am ever reminded we will not become a father to people on the streets or in our neighborhoods because we have yet to bring them to Jesus with true intercession. This is not a recommendation but a command of Holy Scripture: "Pray the Lord of the harvest to send out laborers into His harvest" (Matt. 9:38). Prayer opens the door to people's hearts and brings down the power of God. He did not admonish us to "pray without ceasing" without a reason. After all, the result of asking is receiving; of seeking, finding; and of knocking, having the door opened.

Israel was a visible manifestation of an invisible reality. Adam was a visible manifestation of the invisible God. That is why he was made in the image of God. What Adam represented was the nature and character of the Father. Likewise, this is true about the marriage relationship—it represents what should be happening in the church: a coming together in love resulting in precious new offspring. We see this in the suburbs, but something is missing in the inner cities. We have to go outside of those boundaries and move into the streets and see those little kids as our children and birth them in prayer.

Jesus sees them and says He ever lives to make intercession. We know He is praying people into the kingdom. Hosea 3 relates, "Let us know, . . . Let us pursue the knowledge of the LORD" (Hos. 6:3). The word "know" as it is used here is the same word explaining that Adam "knew" Eve and she conceived. We must understand that it is through prayer that we conceive spiritual children. As in marriage, men and women conceive through union of the marriage covenant, so our relationship with God has to be real and intimate enough so that we are conceiving spiritual children. We can't just take them down the Romans Road and leave them out there in the world as orphans, feeling self-satisfied for how many we have won to Christ that day. Newborns in Christ become our children, and we are responsible to raise them up in the fear and admonition of God. We raise them up with our lives and impart to them the substance of our character. They know who we represent and who they represent, even as a natural father is identified with his children.

The goal of these we nurture is that they become servant-leaders and champions in society. Always remember—kind begets kind. If you don't like the character of your children, you have some self-examination to do. Spiritual children are no different. The elders in the ancient cities stood watch over their areas. They looked for inequities and remedied them. That is the challenge I present to my people: to become willing to go outside the local church proper and look over the cities, become elders over the cities and care for our spiritual children.

I challenge mothers the same way. One does not have to be a natural mother to mother children. You can birth spiritual babies. Most people are aware of the status of a first lady in America. It can be a visible and powerful role. But God has called women to a higher role, that of becoming a first lady in God. A woman of virtue.

This generation of children is being raised in a cesspool of sin. God is calling uncompromising and dedicated men and women who are willing to be crushed, who are willing to be bridges that don't rebel against being walked on, to conceive these precious souls through prayer and love into His family. If it seems impossible, remember God said to Abraham, "for all the land which you see I give to you and your descendants forever" (Gen. 13:15). Imagine Abraham looking all the way to the present day! In Romans 4 it is confirmed that he became the heir of all things. He saw to our generation, and he is still producing children.

Abraham is called the father of faith. Through intercessory prayer we can see beyond ourselves even as God sees. Not with natural eyes, but with spiritual eyes. We need to see this generation, and God will give it to us. How? By being His people and by being brought to a level of truly knowing Him. Too often people talk about what God is trying to do, and they speak about Him in the second person. People easily spot secondhand revelation and devotionless Christians. They are looking for genuine, truly consecrated men and women. Consecration shows.

One such individual, prayer-prepared and consecrated to God and His service, was a rather unknown individual by the name of William Seymour, a black man born into poverty and primitive surroundings. He had a burning desire to know God and become a recipient of all that God had for him and more. He literally hungered and thirsted for righteousness and fed on the bread of life. From his revelations and heart stemmed the roots of millions upon millions of Pentecostal believers. Many researchers believe that Daddy Seymour may be the most important black religious leader in the history of America. Azusa Street was his famous address, but he never sought fame, he sought God.

His message addressed the root of sin and the power and blood of Jesus coming together. He passionately preached that all believers are brothers in the spirit and should not be separated by creed or doctrine.

Race was not an issue, though the man had experienced many of the inequities of the day. Early in his ministry he looked for someplace where he could learn more about Jesus. He enrolled in a Bible class; however, segregation laws forced him to remain outside the room, in the hall, to listen and learn. He was not permitted to be seated with the rest who were studying the Bible.

Instead of letting a root of bitterness grow from being treated so sinfully, he started multiracial prayer groups. He would fast for days to discover the mind of God. The genesis of the Azusa Street revival came from prevailing prayer and a time when he and his group entered into a ten-day fast to find more of God. The result was the outpouring that is recorded in church annals. God chose humble beginnings to accomplish an awesome ministry. Thousands came to Christ. He was a forerunner of worm training. Even during the intensity of his ministry, he was crushed and stepped on by so-called believers.

Daddy Seymour cared for the whole of God's family. He would speak from Genesis 45:19, "Take you wagons out of the land of Egypt for your little ones, and for your wives, and bring your father, and come" (Gen. 45:19, KJV). He would look at his vast audience, many standing outside the wooden building, while others were pressed together so tightly it was hard to breathe, and tell the people that God's spirit impressed him to give a message to everyone. Truly God included everyone; this verse, early in Scripture, is all-inclusive.

In his own unique way he would remind men that God said, "Son, be of good cheer, thy sins be forgiven thee." To women he spoke, "Daughter, be of good comfort; thy faith hath made thee whole." To children, "Suffer the little children to come unto me and forbid them not, for such is the kingdom of God." He would preach that no one is left out of God's call to repentance.

The building of this outpouring in 1906 has been demolished and replaced by a cultural center. Only a signpost remains. However, like Abraham saw the future, I believe

Daddy Seymour's faithfulness has allowed us to be recipients of "the latter-day rain" that he prophesied. Will there be another Azusa Street, another great Welsh revival? Are we willing to take the cross into the street, be subject to the cross fire of the gangs?

Researchers tell us that the growth of cities is twice as fast as the rest of the world's population, and the rate is increasing. It is time to wake up. We need a spiritual awakening. Too long we have been intimidated by society. We have to reverse this kind of thinking and go all out for God. We need to compete in the marketplace. Reconciliation is ours to offer.

People will stop looking to the government for a handout if, when they look to the church, they can get their needs met. I am convinced we can stop welfare right now. It can happen if we bring those on welfare into the church. Currently the federal welfare industry that is grown in Washington, D.C., is the largest industry in the nation. However, the church, which historically administered welfare, has the greatest power in the world.

When blacks came out of slavery, half of the high schools built were paid for by the local places of worship. Every black insurance company came out of the church. Pastors visited the poor, knowing Christ's concern and admonition for them, and brought them to church. They were assured that Christ was the answer to their needs.

That changed in the 1930s with the New Deal of Franklin Roosevelt and in the Great Society programs of the 1960s that we have already mentioned. Now we have so-called pastors who lead people from the doors of the church to the doors of government assistance. See the reversal? Initially we led the people out in the world to the steps of the church because there was spiritual and material provision.

Churches Have Become Caretakers of Ivory Towers Rather Than Caretakers of People

Something changed that caused the church to build ivory towers and become caretakers of those towers rather than of the people. It is the people who were lost sight of and they are our greatest asset. Reconciliation requires total commitment to, consecration to, and selling out to God. It will never happen unless we are willing to be bridges, walked-on bridges, for God.

Changed People Change People

Jesus died for people. The thing that He is now praying for is people. He is going to give all that He owns to people. When are we going to wake up? We are the people whom God wants to use to reach people. We have to change. As we change and get more of God, we can change others. Changed people change people! Others can only be changed by the degree that we ourselves are changed.

I am convinced that a visitation from God is coming, and we are close to it. I look at Daddy Seymour and his prophecy over us and remember Abraham's vision to the ends of the world and I realize that I know their God. The God of Abraham, Isaac, and Jacob is my God. He is the same yesterday, today, and forever. He was crushed as a worm for us so we could be raised to reconcile this world to His Father and to one another.

God has laid on my heart to implore each reader to take God at His word and to take Him seriously. When we really meet Jesus seriously and allow ourselves to be crushed as we model His character, the impact will rock this world.

3

It's Time to Lay Off Uncle Tom

Love your enemies, bless them that curse you, do good to them that hate you, and pray for them which despitefully use you, and persecute you; that ye may be the children of your Father which is in heaven.

Matthew 5:44–45, KJV

*H*undreds of tired students poured out of the classrooms and made their way to the cafeteria. Those who had brought their lunch looked for shady spots under the trees outside the student union. Everyone was talking with friends, studying between bites, or just people watching and enjoying a cup of coffee. Suddenly a piercing voice brought everyone to attention, "Stop acting like dust in the flesh and start acting like Jesus!" The college senior was passionate in his desire to bring racial reconciliation to his campus. He looked intensely at his instant audience. It wasn't the first time he had addressed the crowd of students and in no time the regular picketers showed up. "How do you act like God?" Before he could answer, the picketers began to hurl racial slurs at their "brother." He refused to be intimidated. Over their continuous taunts he called, "Start showing color-blind love and imitate the character of Jesus."

The chants "Down with Jesus" increased. "Down with this white-lovin' bigot." They missed the issue but could not help but "see" his heart had they paused to listen. He kept preaching. The committed senior knew that when sin abounds, grace abounds even more. The aggressive crowd began to close in, but he did not fear for his life; he feared for theirs and their eternal destruction if they would not believe in Jesus. The bold student had discovered Jesus as the uncommon denominator to bring reconciliation to his life and world. He knew and had experienced firsthand, in a racially polarized world, that Christ is the only answer.

He centered his message on the character of Jesus. He presented Jesus as a slave to God. He declared that love is colored red, red as the crimson blood Jesus shed on the cross. The same color as everyone there whether black or white. The issue the brave student used to challenge the group was not color but character, the character of Jesus. As the dedicated young black poured out his heart to the racially mixed group, a crude sign was being constructed curbside: DON'T LISTEN TO UNCLE TOM. HE DOESN'T SPEAK FOR BLACKS.

Why should this ghetto-born black who found Jesus in a storefront Methodist church, soon to graduate with honors and having secured a fine job, subject himself to this kind of harassment? If you could look into his eyes you'd see a reflection of Jesus. God gave him eyes to see and a heart to reach out to the angry and militant with words of reconciliation. The love of Jesus motivated him to seek and to save those who were lost. He had discovered the truth about Christ and those who followed Him. Through his knowledge of the Word he was confident the simmering debates on race would only be resolved through Jesus. He would not be stopped because Jesus would not be stopped. Even death did not silence His voice.

I identify with that courageous young man. I am black and I am a slave, a slave of righteousness. We find ourselves in good company. Paul labeled fellow believers "servants."

Epaphras, who is one of you, a servant of Christ, greets you, always laboring fervently for you in prayers, that you may stand perfect and complete in all the will of God.

Colossians 4:12

The Old Testament reveals that Joseph was sold into slavery by his scheming brothers. Although they had intended nothing but evil, God turned it into something good by placing Joseph in a position to rescue his people during a dire time of famine throughout the land. Who can forget the dramatic story of Shadrach, Meshach, and Abednego as they were spared from the flames in the fiery furnace? Or Daniel, as he influenced the fate of nations through his interpretation of the dreams of Nebuchadnezzar? History is filled with the examples of uncommon people who rose above physical captivity to overcome and bear witness the awesome power of God.

Epithet to Example

During the struggle against slavery, there were certain slaves who had managed a better existence for themselves than their brothers. These blacks were willing to sellout their race in order to stay in the good graces of their owners. They supported the status quo because it meant that they could maintain a position above their brothers who were struggling for freedom. Such slaves would keep the "massa" informed about which slaves might cause him trouble and interfere with his money-making. These privileged few believed they were not their brother's keeper. They used every means of fawning obeisance to advance themselves while others of their race were treated in the most brutal fashion, a situation they were aware of but chose to ignore so as not to jeopardize their position.

As the struggle against oppression raged on, this despicable group of self-serving blacks became the hated few. Because of what had been suffered by the black race, the first wave of freedom eventually brought the inevitable tidal wave of reaction against everything that had the slightest hint of slavery about it. It was in this climate that a novel, which many credit with educating the white man about the inhumanity of slavery, became a symbol of what blacks hate. The book was entitled *Uncle Tom's Cabin*. Now any black who is seen fawning to the white community is automatically labeled an Uncle Tom.

This is a terrible twisting of history that must be corrected. While there were blacks who soldout their race for personal gain, it is a greivous error to fall into the trap of political correctness and misuse the name of Uncle Tom. Sadly, this name is now being twisted even further to denigrate blacks of upstanding moral character. If a student is applying himself in his studies and getting ahead, he is called an Uncle Tom. If a worker puts in some extra hours without pay out of a sense of doing a job well, he is called an Uncle Tom. Only Satan could instigate such twisted thinking. Those who should be held up as examples to follow are ridiculed as if they are the cause of the problems facing the black community.

The time has come to remove the mantle of political correctness from the persona of Uncle Tom and see him in the context of one of God's shining kingdom treasures. There are two standard definitions of Uncle Tom: the elderly black slave who is the main character in the pre–Civil War, antislavery novel, *Uncle Tom's Cabin*, published in 1852, and a black person whose behavior toward whites is regarded as fawning, submissive, or servile.

Many blacks have been taught to hate Uncle Tom and use his name as a symbol of detested compromise with the white man. I, for one, completely disagree. The true attributes of this fictional character are precisely what both blacks and whites need to spark a great awakening. It is time to move Uncle Tom from epithet to example.

According to the plot of *Uncle Tom's Cabin*, a faithful slave, affectionately called Uncle Tom, was separated from his family and sold by a Kentucky slave owner, Mr. Shelby, to pay his debts. Since Tom's conversion to Christianity, he had become one of Shelby's best slaves. While holding church services in his cabin, the youngest Shelby son, George, secretly mentored by Tom in the Christian faith, read aloud from the Bible to the largely illiterate gathering.

After a series of misadventures, Tom becomes the slave of Simon Legree, whose very name has come to mean impulsive cruelty. Tom had knowledge of the whereabouts of two female runaway slaves. Under the law of the time, the penalty for aiding a runaway, even for someone who was free, was severe. Knowing the price he would have to pay, Tom gave up his life to ensure their freedom. Uncle Tom is a Christ figure. Christ paid the ultimate price when He willingly surrendered His life to ensure our freedom from sin and eternal damnation.

Many black brothers may find this difficult to accept, but there are tremendous lessons we can learn from the life and death of Uncle Tom. Instead of being an object of hatred, scorn, and loathing, he should be held high as a black role model whose example in Christ helps set black America free. The true meaning of his life has become lost in a sea of ignorance and reproach. After leading a life in which his faith never wavered, he exhibited Christlike qualities right up to his final breath. He did not fight against his oppressors with fleshly weapons. Like Jesus, he could enter into heaven without regrets or desire for revenge because of his intimate fellowship with the Father.

Tom reflected the glory of God in his suffering and death. Even at the end he was still concerned for his wife's feelings and the salvation of his former master. He prayed the evil Simon Legree would repent so he could enter the kingdom of heaven. Jesus promised the dying thief on the cross eternal life if he repented and then cried, "Father, into Your hands I commit My spirit" (Luke 23:46). Even while suffering an agonizing death, Jesus remained in fellowship with heaven, surrendered to the sovereignty of God. He knew without a doubt God was in control, and His suffering had meaning. The bottom line of His life on earth had only been perfecting Him for eternity.

We do not understand the necessity for suffering nor the benefit from tribulation. In fact, we rebel against it. We resist suffering because we hate the thought of remaining passive in hostile circumstances. In times like these we need a divine perspective. Submission to God is aggressive, not passive. It takes power and incredible resistance to endure pain or oppression and not rise up and fight against it. It takes strength to face your enemies and walk in the spirit of love. It takes perseverance to keep yourself under control and not take revenge. This was the true spirit of Uncle Tom. He epitomized the message in Matthew 5:43–48:

You have heard that it was said, "You shall love your neighbor and hate your enemy." But I say to you, love your enemies, bless those who curse you, do good to those who hate you, and pray for those who spitefully use you and persecute you, that you may be sons of your Father in heaven; for He makes His sun rise on the evil and on the good, and sends rain on the just and on the unjust . . . be perfect, just as your Father in heaven is perfect.

In the story, George Shelby finally locates Tom just before his death. He is appalled at the brutal beating his old mentor endured and tells him he has come to buy him back and take him home. Tom informs him that he's too late. "The Lord's bought me and is going to take me home. Heaven is better than Kintuck. . . . Don't call me poor fellow," said Tom solemnly. "I have been poor fellow; but that's all past and gone now. I'm right in the door, going into glory! Heaven has come! I've got the victory—the Lord Jesus has given it to me!"

Because Tom was filled with the Spirit of the Lord, he was able to transcend his own condition and recognize the eternal priorities of the Lord. Even at the threshold of death's door, he was able to look beyond himself and his circumstances to see another man's spiritual need.

There are tremendous lessons we can learn from the life and death of Uncle Tom. Isn't it odd that, at a time when racial tensions are on the increase, a black role model that could set America free has instead become an object of loathing and ridicule? Such are the tactics in Satan's daily war against God. Black Americans suffering from the slavery of racism should not be offended by whites, but should instead cover them with such a spirit of love and forgiveness that they cease to be offenders. For reconciliation, we must see ourselves as uniquely qualified to use our cruel history as a steppingstone to greatness rather than a stumbling block to keep us down. The very thing blacks hate is actually to their advantage in God's view.

It is imperative that we all, as the body of Christ, learn to go down as it is described in Philippians 2:7–8. The symbolism is unmistakable. As the worm goes down into the earth, so our Lord:

Made Himself of no reputation
Took upon Himself the form of a slave
Was made in the likeness of men
Found in the fashion of a man
Humbled Himself

Became obedient unto death
Even the death of the cross

In so doing He met every demand of His Father, opening wide the door of reconciliation across cultures and nations. In return, God hath highly exalted Him and given Him a name that is above every name. What an example to follow!

We have just read how He made Himself of no reputation. He humbled Himself. If you have not been raised up yet, then you have not gone down far enough into the depths of God's refining process. Because when you do go down, there is an irrefutable law: God will lift you up again in His time.

The liberal press, books, politicians, and opinion spinners talk about the hopelessness of the inner cities and the desperate plight of the black community. Some believe it is the fruit of past wrongs like the reprehensible Jim Crow laws in the South, whites-only drinking fountains, and lynchings—a part of our history that few today comprehend. They question where the civil rights movement was hijacked and why there is so much resentment, division, and welfare dependency. Pouring billions of dollars into programs has not worked. A high percentage of program recipients respond in multiple forms of violence and revenge. Talk of reparations or legislating racial quotas has not brought change. The government insists it cannot legislate morality, but legislation for immorality proliferates.

Respect for authority is vanishing, right along with vanishing values. The hope for change has plunged to its lowest level. In reaching this depth of despair, I believe, having been brought down so low, there is now the potential of rising again. The Bible says, "In the valley of Achor, there is a door of hope" (Josh. 7:24–26). God is a God of breaking through, no matter how dark the day or how high the obstacles.

The Lord is the creator of race. There is no reason for whites in America, or any other culture anywhere in the world, to feel superior. None of us had anything to do with our coming into this world. It was God's idea.

Even in disadvantaged cultures there is no reason for anyone to feel inferior and insecure because Genesis makes clear that "God created man in His image and likeness." Just because our Constitution claims, for the sake of taxation and representation, that a black person was only three-fifths of a person, it does not mean that God changed His mind. His word is sealed in heaven.

What has happened in the black community? They have bought into a philosophy and vision that are not of God. The consequences have been severe. They have been brought low. Now they must come back to the vision of the Lord and seek to walk in the image and likeness of God. When they have been misused by the white community, they can turn what was a stumbling block—being brought low—into a steppingstone toward rising up. Having been forced into slavery, they now can volunteer to become willing slaves of God.

Slavery can be used as an opportunity to say Christ is teaching how to be like Himself. Blacks can take on the Joseph spirit with no guilt, knowing the Lord is preparing them for this very day. From this posture, they can reach out to the white community and the church and become a visible model of how not to be moved out of the character of Christ, even in the midst of suffering. Character, not color, defines destiny.

In the Midst of Suffering, He Refused to Be Moved from the Character of Christ

No matter what we are called to go through, even if it is demeaning, we are challenged to maintain our faithfulness to

God. This very stance and availability to God opens the door for drawing others to Him with the attractiveness of Christ. This is why Uncle Tom is to be held up as an example. Even in the midst of suffering, he refused to be moved out of the character of Christ and chose to lead others to repentance by his example of humility.

Whites, as they look out in repentance, may identify with the sins of the forefathers as Jesus identified with Adam's transgression. Christ did not do anything wrong, but He identified and numbered Himself with the transgressors. As a result, He died as the innocent for the guilty. He came to pay a debt He did not owe, because we owed a debt we could not pay.

If we fail to understand this vital point, we miss God's redemptive purpose in our circumstances. If we refuse to accept this critical truth, we abdicate spirituality. As whites have traditionally been people of advantage, they have often chosen to use people to get more instead of using their resources to raise the standards of others. The Lord says this is visionless, lacking compassion and loving money more than people. Jesus made clear the love of money is the root of evil. When we refuse to use our resources as God ordained, we are ignoring the biblical responsibility of handling wealth.

Why does God give wealth? The answer is clearly stated in His holy Word.

And you shall remember the LORD your God, for it is He who gives you power to get wealth, that He may establish His covenant which He swore to your fathers, as it is to this day.

Deuteronomy 8:18

God gives power to get wealth to establish His covenant. Your wealth is to be used to reach out and win more people to

Him. In the process, and lacking or ignoring biblical teaching, we have allowed the government to take over what God's people should have done with their funds.

In Leviticus and Numbers it states that the tithe is for the strangers, the widows, and the poor within the gates. Rescue missions across the country have a high ratio of changed lives when their programs include Jesus Christ as the way out of the ghetto and homelessness. He modeled His concern for the poor and outcast even as He lived in Capernaum, a place of lepers and wanderers.

> The Spirit of the Lord GOD is upon me, because the LORD has anointed me to preach good tidings to the poor; He has sent me to heal the brokenhearted, to proclaim liberty to the captives, and the opening of the prison to those who are bound; to proclaim the acceptable year of the LORD, . . . To console those who mourn, . . . to give them beauty for ashes, the oil of joy for mourning, the garment of praise for the spirit of heaviness; that they may be called trees of righteousness, the planting of the LORD, that He may be glorified.
>
> Isaiah 61:1–3

Wealth used for God's glory changes welfare dependence to Christ dependence. The bottom line or return on investment from such wise money management is high eternal profit, paying an ongoing interest in changed lives.

> And they shall rebuild the old ruins, they shall raise up the former desolations, and they shall repair the ruined cities, the desolations of many generations.
>
> Isaiah 61:4

We are blessed today to reclaim that opportunity. We own the resources and have been given an opportunity to build the kingdom. If we use our wealth to establish God's covenant, the lost and disheartened will run to the church because there they will not be sent away. There they will find as God designed—a place of peace and rest. If the church is not the center for racism breakthroughs, it won't happen anywhere else. If the church, possessing the knowledge and love of Christ, is not willing to be broken before God, the beautiful fragrance of racial reconciliation will not fill our homes and places of worship. God has given the church the responsibility to spread His message of hope. Jesus knows there is tribulation in this world, but He declares, "be of good hope, I have overcome the world."

Martin Luther King Jr. applied the gospel to past disgrace and atrocities imposed on the black community. His agenda was nonviolent civil disobedience in order to bring political and social change. Jesus steps forward with His compelling presentation: there is but one way, one model, to revive the soul of the nation. Life-changing decisions must come from the inside out. Jesus wants us to model that life change to a watching world through how we love one another and how we respond to the sinful acts of racism, just like Uncle Tom.

Driven Down to Be Raised Up

I cannot overemphasize that if you have not been raised up yet, you have not gone down far enough. God is zealous to raise up people, leaders, and heroes, but godly advancement is based on your humility in Christ.

The Christian media of the world tends to hold up the wrong models for reaching the lost. The rich and beautiful, athletes or stars who have enjoyed a little success, are held high. It is rare that ordinary, struggling, everyday mothers and fathers, laborers, and scriptural "rope holders" make magazine covers or are examples from pulpits on Sunday mornings.

Somehow our standards have come to look a lot like the world's. Christian publicity is driven by glitter and glamour. The pedestal gets ever higher and in many cases is far beyond the true spiritual character of those placed on it. Time and again, rank-and-file Christians are set up for a fall. This totally mismodels the kingdom. Why? Because all the glitz and hype has taken the focus away from Jesus Christ, the author and finisher of our faith. Jesus is the refiner of our souls, Jesus alone. This is why Uncle Tom is an example to follow. He made himself so small that all you could see in his life was Jesus Christ. Even as God gave Adam a choice, Joshua issued a challenge to "choose this day whom you will serve."

Example Isn't Just One Thing, It Is Everything

I look back to those in history who were faithful and thank God for their example. Example is not just one thing, it is everything. Early in the nineteenth century when America was still young, the right of the individual was paramount and the overall consensus was, because of our spiritual heritage, each person would make the right choice. This was a century before the Puritan ethic (that man was insignificant, puny, and sinful) prevailed.

The westward movement gained momentum and with it came the evil of slavery. One family, through several generations, became models of change. Born in 1775, Lyman Beecher was a renowned clergyman. His seven sons followed him into the ministry. Their combined courage left a spiritual trail of service, temperance, mission societies, and social change.

After the death of his mother, Lyman was sent to live with an aunt and uncle in what some today would describe as a dysfunctional family. The family's reverence for God was strict, and Lyman was allowed to play on the sabbath only after "three stars appeared in the sky." Their library consisted of two books, the Bible and a psalm book.

He was glad to escape the rigidity and farm life and went to school at Yale. There he met Englishmen who had experienced freedom from legalism, unknown to him at the time. It was an era when Thomas Paine's *Age of Reason* was widely distributed. For a time, he followed along with them. However, when Jonathan Edward's grandson became president of the institution, Yale was restored to Calvinist theology and Puritan living. In the process he had a great influence on Lyman.

This president of Yale modeled Christ and became, as young Lyman described, "one I love as my own soul and he loved me as a son." Through his influence, Lyman entered the ministry. Later, discouraged by the apathy of his church, he wrote his wife, "immortal souls are sleeping on the brink of hell." Descriptive words of many places of worship today.

He persevered and in 1800 a revival broke out among his church people. As a result he was thrust into national recognition. Historians record that in 1818 Connecticut officially disestablished religion, making church membership an individual choice and thereby ending the required payment of the church tithe. At the time Beecher called it the darkest day in the history of Connecticut. Later he came to feel "it was good for the church because it threw them wholly on their own resources and on God."

Lyman Beecher was a strong father. He taught his children in an atmosphere enriched by parental affection and a sense of their own worth in the sight of God. Beecher's children were raised to know they had a place of destiny in God's plan. Of the eleven of his children who lived to maturity, the most well known are Henry Ward Beecher and Harriet Beecher Stowe.

Henry was influenced by Calvin Stowe, who later became his brother-in-law. Calvin exemplified God as a living, vital, available presence. Through him, Henry saw Christ as the light of the world and lost mankind in need of a savior. Henry wrote, "From that hour I felt that God had a father's heart, that Christ loved me in my sin, and cared for me with unutterable tenderness." Preaching the love and tenderness of God catapulted him to great influence. He preached truth. One of his parishes grew from nine to two thousand. At first avoiding the issue of slavery, he was slow to identify with the abolitionists, believing that slavery would cease if its spread was prevented. He felt that uplifting and educating slaves to become good Christians would force their masters to be inspired or shamed to free them. That hope proved not to be the solution.

Time and prayer changed his mind on the issue. Slavery was deplorable, he proclaimed, except when a man became a slave of Christ. Because of his new commitment to the cause, born of travailing prayer, Abraham Lincoln invited him to appear with him in support of the Thirteenth Amendment abolishing slavery. It was Beecher, in the closing days of the war, who gave the address at the ceremony returning the flag to Fort Sumter after the South's surrender.

Beecher had trials and personal testings, but "the end was the beginning of going to glory, and being allowed to step into the holy presence of God." He conveyed that to friends, teaching his children God's wrath and love was a duty of every father. If obedience was not learned in the home, there would never be obedience and allegiance to Father God.

Harriet Beecher Stowe was the sixth of the Beecher children. Her father regretted the birth of a daughter, but God decides who comes into this world. Raised by a grandmother, she became an avid reader, loving Lord Byron and great poetry. At the age of thirteen she went to live with her sister, a teacher.

She taught at the academy when she was fourteen. Questions about her belief in God led to some insecurities. After her marriage to Calvin Stowe, her home was in Cincinnati, a gateway to the South. Here her tender heart was touched by the plight of the slave society. She witnessed the burning of black homes, one among many injustices and ugly incidents. Even though three-quarters of the three thousand blacks in the city were former slaves who had won their freedom, they were not truly free. The Bible opened to her the truth that being lowly leads to the highest position of learning to be a bond slave of God.

In Cincinnati, the Reverend John Rankin, who assisted runaway slaves through the Underground Railroad, influenced her thinking. When she and her husband learned a freed slave girl they had hired was being sought by her former master, the issue was brought into their living room. The passage of the Fugitive Slave Law in 1850 mandated intense punishment for those who harbored escapees.

Harriet began writing a series of articles for an antislavery magazine which evolved into the novel *Uncle Tom's Cabin*. The inspiration for the book came from a vision of "unusual intensity." Reading the story to her own children caused them to become incensed by the cruelty of slavery. Later, her husband, in absorbing her words, insisted that it was imperative for her to complete the story as the Lord had intended.

To this day, it is said that Harriet Beecher Stowe's little book, more than anything else, was the catalyst responsible for the Civil War and was the premier portrayal of the central moral issue in the conflict over slavery.

God led her to design her main character to "explode the legend of happy, thoughtless, insensitive darkies," the picture slaveholders loosely held up as the lives of their "contented" slaves. She emphasized the power of Christian faith, and her closing words to churches need to be heeded as we move toward another century: "Stop protecting injustice, cruelty and sin lest they bring on themselves the wrath of an angry God."

Her father, Lyman, is described as a priest and a prophet of the old school of Puritanism, intent on saving souls and fixing their thoughts on the life to come. His children were social servants and reformers. A godly mix is the crying need of this day, leading men to a preoccupation with God and confronting man's inhumanity to man.

Families like the Beechers of yesterday challenge me to bring up my children as children of God. Giving them wholly to God and preparing them for the kingdom cannot be overemphasized. We must lovingly rule with godliness in our homes to rule unitedly in the kingdom to come.

I must refer back to the intent of *Uncle Tom's Cabin*. In my mind just now the scene recurs as Simon Legree starts cursing, spitting venom with his words. Tom answers the wrath, "Oh, I would that he would give his life to God, but I fear that he would not." I think of Jesus, nailed to a cross with criminals on each side, saying, "Father, forgive them for they know not what they do." Jesus' spirit had permeated Tom. The spirit by which He lived covered this slave as he was about to die. In an opposite spirit, he was praying that those who were destroying him would have life. Standing by was George, Shelby's youngest son, who had been affected and mentored by Tom's life. When George relates that he is not eager to see men like Simon Legree in heaven, Tom contradicts him saying, "Hush, you mustn't talk like that."

A slave who did not have an ounce of slave mentality showed himself to be a stalwart slave of God. Even at the point of death Tom was telling a man who had freedom, education, and privilege that he could raise his standards beyond himself and think at the kingdom level, even as Tom had been translated to a higher level of relationship with God.

The Black Community Must Stop Criticizing Uncle Tom

I want to boldly affirm Tom. The black community must stop criticizing Uncle Tom. He is a role model who, when he was stepped on like a worm, at the point of crisis, evidenced the nature of the classic, model worm, Jesus. When one says Uncle Tom sold out, how about placing that statement introspectively into your own life. Instead of selling out to people and worldly philosophies, sell out in terms of your commitment to Christ. Sell out until there is nothing of you left, not the domination of your culture, not your coloring, not your gender, not your denomination. You stand up to live only for Jesus. It does not matter what you are going through. The issue is, are you evidencing Christ in the circumstances you are in. That is the message of the Bible. That is the message of Jesus. Imagine being so sold out for Jesus. He went through hell on earth, but He lived and walked in heaven's domain. Walking with Him are the faithful Uncle Toms, living out their kingdom destiny.

Blacks Have Had 250 Years of Slave Qualification

Jesus talked to His disciples about being servants. Now blacks in America have slavery as the very essence of their history. The Lord says, if you are willing, you can have an early start to reigning in the kingdom by becoming a slave of God today.

Blacks have had more than two centuries of training in being a slave of man. It can be added as long-term qualification to prepare them to be a fine slave of God or to rule as a king. They are uniquely positioned to be kept and used in this last day until Jesus returns as king for the feast of in-gatherings. If they know how to redemptively look at their past and use the training for present service, then in that serving they will become future kings and leaders. That is the heart of Jesus' message.

Every one of the apostles was a slave. Look back at the prophets. They referred to themselves as servants. He clarified their responsibility by informing them that they were going to rule with Him, but they also were going to have to suffer with Him. Suffering is reign preparation. It does not matter what race you belong to, the same standard holds true. Consider Israel. They all went through bondage and slavery because God had chosen them. The Lord asked, "Why did I choose you?" Watch this!

Jacob had to be converted from a snake to a worm. Out of his conversion and life, he produced Joseph. Joseph was sent into slavery and soon thrown into prison. But God raised him up and blessed him greatly. After fourteen years when his brothers came to him in physical famine, he made an "Uncle Tom" statement: "You cannot do anything to me, the Lord sent me here, brought me 'down' to prepare you for this day." His imprisonment and bondage were preparation and training to become second in command over all Egypt.

If the black community would embrace this magnificent truth, it would change the world. Real strength, power, and leadership comes from servanthood.

The Lord spoke a similar message about Israel in Deuteronomy 8. "I chose you, not because you are the greatest of all, but because you are the fewest of all people." He proved to them as He does to us this hour, man shall not live by bread alone. Exodus 19 is a message to Israel, "I bore you on eagle's wings that I might bring you to myself." Translated: Israel's delivery from slavery was not the Lord bringing them into the land of promise. It was the Lord's using their physical circumstances as a picture of what He was really doing—bringing them unto Himself. The very words should have provoked within those Israelites an intense desire to plead to God to come upon them.

The black community still looks for a white man, a government, a Farrakhan, to be their deliverer. They, by and large, remain unbroken. The Lord is not going to allow any man to become their deliverer. Jesus Himself is the only deliverer. Only as they become broken and their cry becomes God-centered and Jesus-centered rather than politically centered will the Lord come and heal their broken, fragmented lives and deliver them.

He will then impart their destiny in Him. While they should be missionaries, they are still a mission field. They need a new vision of the Lord of the breaking through.

The Israelites became broken. They cried to be liberated from their taskmasters. The Lord sent Joseph down to them to be the seed of the right spirit to the nation. After more than four centuries of slavery, Moses became the man God chose to bring them out. Moses had been broken and became as a worm. After forty years of testing, he realized he could not handle the situation in his own strength. He became the seed of a whole people who could give credit for their deliverance only to God. Yet because of their unwillingness to have His seed of truth planted into their lives, they died in the wilderness. God does not play church. He is the church.

God Does Not Play Church, He Is the Church

I fear the same will happen to those who do not receive the good seed God wants to plant in every life. I believe at present many in the black community are experiencing death and destruction in their own wilderness because they will not allow His seed to be planted in their lives. That is why the statistics recording abortion, crime, suicide, sterilization, and imprisonment continue to climb. These sins are a direct result of no one leading them to the steps of the altars of God. Instead they have been left on the front porch of the White House. It is time to recognize the truth. The answers aren't inside. Government has replaced God. God has warned us, "Cursed is the man who makes his flesh his ark." The good news is still on the front pages of God's book. There is an ark of safety for all who will enter in. A place where God is and waits for our decision.

Harriet Beecher Stowe wrote words we have sung in worship services.

> Still, still with Thee, when purple morning
>   breaketh,
> When the bird waketh, and the shadows flee;
> Fairer than morning, lovelier than daylight,
> Dawns the sweet consciousness, I am with Thee.
> So shall it be at last, in that bright morning,
> When the soul waketh, and life's shadows flee;
> On, in that hour, fairer than daylight dawning,
> Shall rise the glorious thought, I am with Thee.

"Still, still with Thee," in the midst of turmoil and transition is possible. The psalmist wrote, "Be still, and know that I am God" (Ps. 46:10). Isn't it interesting that the clauses that compose this Scripture are so interwoven that each may be the cause and each may be the effect of the other. The way to know God is to be still and the way to be still is to know God. This presents one of the most beautiful reciprocities that we find between duty and privilege. The way to do the duty is to accept the privilege, and the way to enjoy the privilege is to do the duty.

So it is being slaves of God. Duty and privilege come together with divine connection, and we have the glorious confidence, "I am with Thee," affirmed by His forever response, and "I am with you always."

4

The Road to Reconciliation

And all things are of God, who hath reconciled us to himself by Jesus Christ, and hath given to us the ministry of reconciliation; to wit, that God was in Christ, reconciling the world unto himself, not imputing their trespasses unto them; and hath committed unto us the word of reconciliation.

2 Corinthians 5:18–19, KJV

*E*ver since the formation of our country there have been calls by blacks for separation from whites. Those voices are increasing despite the billions of dollars spent on social programs designed to counteract race-based discrimination. Our nation has never been more polarized on racial issues than in this generation. Even with decades of effort, the chasm of misunderstanding grows. Tension and division surface and the hope for a color-blind society fades while a new emphasis on color predominates. No longer is the move for integration attracting great marches. The banners being raised today celebrate segregation. The centuries-old quest for inclusion into the mainstream of white society is fading and a new quest for separation is gaining momentum.

At a time when middle-class blacks are more financially secure than ever, they are choosing to move to all-black residential neighborhoods. With bussing and other attempts to integrate schools are falling short of intended goals, there is a rising number of racially separate, private schools. The void and distance between the races is deepening, and the hope that people of all colors will someday be blended on a universal palette of acceptance seems futile.

In 1995 the country was astonished that a man like Louis Farrakhan, a separatist, could rally several hundred thousand black men to come together to demonstrate their connection to each other. But the message of atonement that Farrakhan spoke of was two thousand years too late. Jesus is the only one who is qualified to atone for mankind's sin.

Is Farrakhan a face of reconciliation? In no sense of the word. But he sees a hunger for meaning and is out there trying to fill that void with his brand of racism. Is he a savior of the endangered black male? No. Has he used his oratorical skills to bring peace or nonviolence? No. He refuses to speak out against hate, racism, and anti-Semitism and makes every attempt to manipulate young people.

Hatemongers come in all colors, and bigotry knows no ethnic boundaries. In these last times I believe there will be a proliferation of men like him who are antichrist and have the antichrist spirit. I am appalled but not surprised.

Some well-meaning people have tried to put the best face on this movement, but we must be wary of the implications of the Washington march. The hate-filled aggressive agenda was couched in the language of religion. Well-known terms such as *atonement, fasting, prayer,* and *holy day* drew in many unsuspecting people.

But Farrakhan has set his face against almighty God because he preaches that Jesus was merely a prophet and not the Son of God and savior of mankind. No born-again Christian could join in this movement. Light has no fellowship with darkness. If the issue was only civil, social, or economic, there could be merit. We know this isn't the case. This event was promoted as a religious coming together. I would like to ask Farrakhan,

"Who is your savior?" I would like to ask him if he believes in reconciliation with whites.

Louis Farrakhan and the Nation of Islam are diametrically opposed to Christianity. Elijah Muhammad says of Christianity:

> It is a religion organized and backed by the white devils for the purpose of making slaves of black mankind.
>
> He [Allah] said that Christianity was organized by the white race and they placed the name of Jesus on it as being the founder and author to deceive black people into accepting it.
>
> Once the so-called Negroes drop the religion of slavery [Christianity] and accept Allah for their God and his religion [Islam], Allah will remove their fear and grief, and they will not fear and grieve any more.
>
> He [Jesus] was only a prophet like Moses and the other prophets and had the same religion [Islam]. He did his work and is dead like others of his time, and has not knowledge of their prayers to him.
>
> It is far more important to teach separation of the blacks and whites in America than prayer. Teach and train the blacks to do something for self in the way of uniting and seeking a home on this earth that they can call their own. There is no such thing as living in peace with white Americans.

They are opposed to reconciliation among blacks and whites and even hold to the bizarre belief that white people are devils created by an evil scientist named Yacub.

Such marches led by Farrakhan have been condemned openly as well as endorsed, but the questions from my heart that I have to ask of the Christians who supported him are: Is there any limitation or qualification that you will set regarding a person's beliefs or lifestyle that would prohibit you from following him? Is there anything that will offend your Christian faith enough to force you to forsake black unity? By supporting this march, many proved that their answer to both of these questions is a hearty no.

Our Problem in This Nation Isn't a Skin Problem, It's a Sin Problem

The church, the body of Christ, must model reconciliation through confession, repentance, forgiveness, and restoration. I am convinced that reconciliation can only begin in the church. It must become a living organism of the word, and the work of reconciliation will begin to challenge the stereotypes and open lines of communication. Our problem in this nation is not a skin problem, but a sin problem. We have gained the potential for reconciliation by the blood of Christ but haven't practiced reconciling our hearts to each other. We may have come over on different boats, but we are in the same boat now and it is adrift on a sea of hate.

Jesus spoke, backing His words with His life, death, and resurrection:

> You have heard that it was said, You shall love your neighbor and hate your enemy. But I say to you, love your enemies, bless those who curse you, do good to those who hate you, and pray for those who spitefully use you and persecute you, that you may be sons of your Father in heaven; for He makes His sun rise on the evil and on the good, and sends rain on the just and on the unjust. . . . Be perfect, just as your Father in heaven is perfect.
>
> Matthew 5:43–48

Jesus invites Farrakhan and his followers to repent and come to Him, the true source of revelation and freedom. What is not accomplished through revelation will bring more tribulation. Jesus said, "In the world you will have tribulation; but be of good cheer, I have overcome the world" (John 16:33).

The Inner City: Where Is the Church?

A great fear grips the church when it comes to answering a Macedonian call leading to the ravaged inner cities. Streets are ruled by gangs because there have been too few individuals willing to step into the hellholes and establish ministries like Gangs to Grace.

With the pillars of reconciliation disintegrating, hard facts bring harsh reality. Questions I often ask black youth are "Are you waiting for another Martin Luther King Jr. or are you going to become one yourself?" "Do you want the church to do your work or are you willing to roll up your sleeves and become the church?" "What are you doing to stem the bitterness on the street where lives are wasted hourly?" The only hope is through the One who said, "Be ye reconciled to God" (2 Cor. 5:20, KJV).

In 2 Corinthians, the Lord gives two views of the ministry of reconciliation:

Now all things are of God, who has reconciled us to Himself through Jesus Christ, and has given us the ministry of reconciliation, that is, that God was in Christ reconciling the world to Himself, not imputing their trespasses to them, and has committed to us the word of reconciliation. Now then, we are ambassadors for Christ, as though God were pleading through us; we implore you on Christ's behalf, be reconciled to God.

2 Corinthians 5:18–20

The order here is fascinating, because in the last verse we are told to be ambassadors, in the first verse we are charged to the ministry of reconciliation, and in the middle verse the word of reconciliation appears.

Reconciliation Is Something to Do

What is being emphasized is that reconciliation is something to do. The word of reconciliation is something to say. We usually think of it as the opposite. We say before we do. But the biblical order is doing before saying.

Jesus came into the world before He spoke. His doing preceded His saying. The foundation for reconciliation with others rests on our vertical relationship with the Lord, meaning we have been restored back to the Lord Himself. Jesus became this model. We must be reconciled to God before we can be reconciled to each other.

Even though the media chose to sidestep what was happening, one of the leading groups in changing the scene of apartheid in South Africa was its churches, not secular institutions. Long before the wall of apartheid fell, South African churches modeled integration and reconciliation. This was true in the Azusa Street revival mentioned before as the birthplace of Pentecostalism in America. The color line was broken, similar to what happened at Pentecost in Acts 2. People coming together because Jesus made it clear, We are one.

William Seymour, the black patriarchal figure of Azusa Street felt that one evidence of the baptism of the Holy Spirit was, not speaking in tongues, but unity. The result was people flocking from all over the world to a ghetto in Los Angeles. People from different denominations and races participated in a move of God. It can happen again!

Let's look at some very practical things in this area. When we commit to the Lord, we establish a vertical relationship with Him. However, when it comes to practicing that commitment, we establish horizontal relationships—brother to brother, sister to sister. We work out our vertical commitment horizontally.

When You Pray, You Move Your Feet

So we ask ourselves, What are the basics of working it out and being reconciled one to another? The first and primary basis is unconditional love. Agape love—and God has the only supply available. The second is compassion, or mercy. With unconditional love and compassion as the foundation, we are then prepared to move into the action steps. As the Puritans said, "When you pray, you move your feet." So the first thing we need to do can be written in six little words: Find a need and fill it. We must focus on what this nation needs, but the same principles apply to any nation.

If our only perspective is a historical perspective, then the point of offense becomes the focus. It is important we go back to the place where the offense was initiated. I like to call it the gate. Gates are significant. There are gateways to poverty and gateways to prosperity. Gates are for protection and for rejection. The elders sat in a gate in the Old Testament because those were the places of entry into the city. That was the center of conversation and commerce. Then as now, we find that every disagreement has a beginning. To experience true reconciliation, it is important to go back to the place where that offense originated.

It may be more than a generation back. You ask, How can I get there? Where do I learn the root of the situation? You can go by research done through organizations, talk to relatives, ask where their relatives came from and begin the search.

Traveling by research is still a trip of progress and often uncovers a city of origin or family that can move you to the very place where the disagreement occurred. There you identify with the hurt. Jesus modeled this with Adam.

We are all familiar with stories of feuding families, such as the McCoys and Hatfields. Resentment had been passed down for generations, but no one could define its source. Finally, an old man provided the truth, and he had learned it from another generation.

In finding the source of the hurt, you repent for that person. John Dawson, in his book *Healing America's Wounds*, called this identificational repentance. I hear whites and others saying when this subject is discussed, "I wasn't there. I didn't do anything." Such statements reveal the attitude of Cain. These are common remarks that hold no weight with Jesus and should be disregarded by committed Christians. We *are* our brother's keeper. Jesus went back to where Adam transgressed and sinned against the Father. Jesus was innocent, but He identified with Adam's wrongdoing. We are called to willingly do the same thing and follow His model.

Jesus Was Innocent but He Identified with Adam's Wrongdoing

You have to become as a worm in this because if you cling to your pride or try to protect yourself by not being identified with your forefathers, then you hinder the process of reconciliation. We must be willing to model Jesus. Repentance does not come easy. But after repentance, victory rushes in.

Another point to ponder is to see if anything has been stolen. The Old Testament standard is that if a person had offended or stolen from another, the penalty was repayment plus another 20 percent. Restitution was a big issue. Knowing the injustices and broken promises of the past, the issue of restitution remains large. It was said that you have to understand that if you can benefit from the wealth of your family, you must also face bearing the penalty of the poverty, whether it is spiritual or natural poverty. One cannot be one-sided in this. Blessed are the balanced. This is not right-wing or left-wing thinking. You cannot fly on one wing.

Restitution, as seen in Acts 3:19–22, is the same word for restoration. In reflecting on this, it is restoration spiritually, but there is also a restoration that God required in the Old Testament. What is the basis of it? In the Old Testament it was law. In the New Testament it is love. Why do it? Because it is who you are in Christ. Any way you can heal the hurts of the past you seed in the fruit of repentance. Go back to the place where the reproach was made.

The faces of reconciliation are not only those in other cultures, but it is also true of a husband being reconciled with his wife. He may have hurt her, and it has been going on for several days. Then he comes to clear the air and repent to her. How wonderful it is if a demonstration of his sincerity comes with that repentance! Something beyond mere words that adds yet another measure. I want to go beyond what is required when it comes to repentance and give more than words. In so doing, I have seeded more than is required. It is natural proof that I really mean this act and trust will be restored in time. That is what restitution is all about.

A forgotten reality is resurfacing in this conflict. The Lord is the creator of race and the solution to racial problems. He is the source of destiny.

I had a young black tell me he could only find his true identity by going back to the places of the marches of the 1960s. I suggested he go further. So we talked about the days of Lincoln, the Emancipation Proclamation, and places in Africa where his roots were. But I said that was not far enough. We moved back to Noah. I told him that still was not far enough. He was sure that going back to Adam was the end of the trail. When I said no, he was puzzled and ready to listen. No one had told him that God had a plan for mankind in place before the foundation of the world. We have always been in the bosom of the Father. That is the defining place. The Book of Genesis makes clear that God created man in His image and likeness.

Blacks who know the Lord have a great advantage today. Many have been raised by godly black men and women in the years since the Civil War. However, their conversions are often from the root of generations of faithful slaves who reacted to their circumstances knowing that God was seeing them in their bondage but still found freedom to know Jesus.

Luke 19 is the familiar narrative about Zacchaeus. He was a tax collector, working for the IRS of his day. People were upset when Jesus chose to go to his house, but Jesus was a friend of sinners. He saw the change in Zacchaeus' heart leading him to promise that if he had stolen anything from the people, then he would return it fourfold. Jesus was resembling the brothers when He affirmed the despised tax collector, "I'm wit chew, man!"

Zacchaeus displays the heart of someone really impacted by Jesus. His heart was so changed that he desired to heal the past hurts and wrongs he had inflicted on people. That comes out of love and compassion. No one forced him to change. Jesus' love compelled him to action. His turnaround had nothing to do with affirmative action. Our actions cannot be mandated through the flesh or law. In our heart we have to care about those who are poor, downtrodden, and disadvantaged, so that we become instruments for change in the Lord's hand.

The process of reconciliation is initiated by taking action. Just as love is something you do, so is reconciliation. You begin by developing relationships. If you are in a suburban church, reach out to an urban one. Share services and programs and prayer. I encourage you to establish reconciliation fellowship groups where black and white Christians can live out the vision of walking in fellowship with one another. Assist one another to the level of ability and resources.

The dining table is a place to invite people of other races and learn about one another. Psalm 23 says, "Thou preparest a table before me." It is a place to break bread and break down prejudices. The table of the Lord celebrates His being broken for us. What a blessing to share yours with others and minister reconciliation. Doing this makes you an amazement to others for the sake of Jesus. Being invited is a place of acceptance. The Lord invited us to come and dine, and we are headed for the marriage feast of the Lamb. The home is to model what the kingdom looks like according to Deuteronomy 11:18–21. Asking someone into your home is sharing the atmosphere of heaven. Home environments may be different, but with Jesus present there will be a feast. Some of the most wonderful experiences I have had have been in humble homes where a poverty of funds was obvious but there was a lavish spirit.

You Don't Have to Wait for Someone Else to Repent

> So I returned, and considered all the oppressions that are done under the sun; and behold the tears of such as were oppressed, and they had no comforter; and on the side of their oppressors there was power; but they had no comforter.
>
> *Ecclesiastes* 4:1, KJV

I want to lovingly remind the black community that they have the power to release. In other words, they do not have to wait for the white community to repent. We can initiate forgiveness. We can reach out to the white community and offer them unconditional love, regardless of what they did, because that is what Jesus did for us. We seek to serve them with the servant experience we have had, misappropriated in the past, but now compelled by the love of Christ.

Blacks may not have the cumulative finances of whites, but they show they are serious by developing a greater work ethic. Volunteering to do things lets them know you are aware that you have been labeled lazy and irresponsible in the past, but times are changing. Gain a new sense of confidence and out-work those around you.

When I first went into pastoring, I volunteered to work with a white-owned, successful carpet cleaning company. Wanting to learn the business, I offered to work for no salary. I worked circles around the others. When it came time to start my own business, the proprietor offered to assist me. I learned how to be a producer. I had gotten past the problem of racism in my own mentality. I had reached out and served someone else, and in so doing I became a valuable asset to the company and ensured my own future success.

Write letters to people of other races and tell them how you love them and how God changed your life. Reaffirm what Christ has done for you and release levels of bondage that may still be there.

The Proof of Your Christianity Is Whether You Can Part with What You Have Been Given

I believe the black community is a mission field. They should be our great missionaries, yet they need mentoring and educating. Whether you're black or white, make a commitment to take someone who may not be where you are spiritually, lift them up by your example and seed the truth into their life. The proof of your Christianity is whether or not you can part with what you have been given. That is what Christ did for me and for you. In reality, we rejected Him. And look at this! He gave us His life and has mentored us, developed us, and discipled us into what we are. He is not yet finished with us.

The story is told of two people sitting across a table from one another. There is food on their plates, but the silverware is too long for them to get the food to their own mouth. For both to eat, they have to feed one another. The white community can feed the black community repentance and blessings. The black community can feed the white community forgiveness, acceptance, and unconditional love. Both have something that each needs.

I will always come back to the kingdom meaning. The Lord reigns because He is the creator of everything. Our destiny is wrapped up in what was in the mind of God before the world was made. On the sixth day, He created man and told man what he was created for. Man was inside the kingdom (Eden). When Adam sinned he was kicked out of the kingdom. Jesus Christ came and instead of us immediately going to be with the Father, the kingdom comes into us. Jesus said, "The kingdom of God is within you." It was all part of God's plan before the foundation of the earth.

That is why Paul talks about being an apostle formed in his mother's womb. He was in the mind of God before his birth. By the Lord Jesus coming into our hearts, we have that eternal nature, that nature which takes us back to the beginning of what was in the heart of God. Faith not only allows us to believe for the future, but connects us with the past. From before creation God knew what our circumstances would be. In that context, we are called to apply to our lives today the kingdom principles we are learning under the reign of God.

Francis Schaeffer was one who helped us with the application of kingdom principles to every sphere of life. The Puritans preached it. The early apostles taught it. The rule of God came through the prophets that was still only a shadow of how it would have been in Adam. In the midst of it all, Jesus came to make a way that the Father's domain could come to us, and we could be His representatives on earth. The principles of Christ are the foundation stones for whatever we are called to accomplish in life, and we have been called to model the kingdom. But that cannot be done unless we are willing to be reconciled to each other.

We have been honored to be called sons and daughters of God and privileged to be ministers of reconciliation. As in school, those who are given the assignment will be held accountable to the one who gave the assignment.

In John 15, Jesus says,

Henceforth I call you not servants; for the servant knoweth not what his lord doeth: but I have called you friends; for all things that I have heard of my Father I have made known unto you. Ye have not chosen me, but I have chosen you, and ordained you, that ye should go and bring forth fruit, and that your fruit should remain: that whatsoever ye shall ask of the Father in my name, he may give it you. These things I command you, that ye love one another.

John 15:15–17, KJV

It may seem as though that last statement was an interjection, but it is the foundation of what came before, the standard of a true believer.

Contract or Covenant?

There is a difference between a covenant and a contract. A contract is based upon distrust; a covenant is based upon trust. One limits freedom, the other gives freedom in advance. Jesus said He was not treating us as servants or slaves but rather as friends. Remember when young kids used to prick their fingers, then as a trickle of blood appeared they would clasp hands and swear friendship forever? Jesus said that He would covenant to give His life for us. The difference is that He was shedding His own blood and we could not reciprocate.

With the Lord, the covenant is confirmed by confession. As we confess, the convicting power of the Holy Spirit witnesses to the blood of Jesus and what He has done for us. In Matthew 10:32, Jesus says that He confesses us before the Father. He initiated a covenant with us. He handpicked us. We have an opportunity not only to be saved but to be His disciples.

We should be so amazed by this reality that we say, "God forgive me for rejecting Jesus, for not accepting His full message of reconciliation, for believing I could be reconciled to God and estranged from my brothers in Christ."

If we examine deep down in our hearts, every one of us has a divine sense that God's destiny is wrapped up inside us. He has not only called us but helps by giving us the Holy Spirit. He will abide with us forever.

> When the Comforter is come, whom I will send to you from the Father, even the Spirit of truth [reality], which proceedeth from the Father, he shall testify of me.
>
> *John* 15:26

That is the greatest thing: to know we have been chosen and He has not left us alone. He is giving us privileged information. He says, "I am with you, urging you to reach out and touch people as I have touched you."

Your life has destiny written all over it! We have been handpicked by God to be used to impact our generation. He modeled that out in His own life and with His disciples.

Through rebirth we become the fruit of the disciple's faithfulness and so on down through the generations. We have not been chosen just to receive but to give also, to reach out and bear fruit. Wherever you go and wherever you are, God is with you. Jesus is with you. We need to reaffirm who we are in Christ. Remember, the Lord in choosing Moses said, "Surely, I will be with you."

Heartening to me is a new willingness, even eagerness to reach out and address racial issues and move toward reconciliation. One of the leaders in this has been the Southern Baptist Convention, the largest Protestant denomination in the United States. Their convention approved a historic document on race resolution 219 years after the Declaration of Independence stated that all men are created equal. "This was unfinished business with our African-American brothers and sisters which we needed to address forthrightly and proactively," observed Richard Land. One of the focal points was that of repentance. He further said, "Our ultimate goal should be the eradication of racism in our churches, our Convention, and our country."

I applaud their Resolution on Racial Reconciliation and am humbled by the offer of their publishing arm, Broadman & Holman, to accept this book. I believe God will reward them, and I seed blessing and prosperity into these men of God. The complete resolution is found in the appendix.

The Forty-sixth General Council of the Assemblies of God in Saint Louis, Missouri, on August 12, 1995, voted to adopt a resolution calling for the fellowship to enhance and accelerate efforts toward inclusiveness of black brothers and sisters throughout the General Council. General Superintendent Thomas E. Trask pledged, "that with the Spirit's enablement, I will do all within my power to fulfill what this General Council has called for. I support this action with all my heart." The complete text of the revised resolution is also found in the appendix.

God is impressing His church to reconcile itself to the hurtful pain and prejudice of the past and to live in the truth that we are one in Christ.

I am often asked what the church has lost and what is it that America gropes to find. I believe what has been lost is the model for living like Christ and, in turn, reaching out to others, looking for opportunities to be a servant.

We will continue to be trapped in the issues of race and color as long as we have a mind-set based on cultural differences. Jesus shows us that you do not reach a nation with culture, you reach a nation with character, the character of Christ.

I sum up this issue with a statement from my heart. If I had a choice of being where my race is as opposed to being where grace is, I would choose grace every time. It is the grace of God that brings salvation. The will of God will never lead me where the grace of God will not intercede for me. Grace begets graciousness and fills the heart with gratitude to God. He sees us as one in the bond of His love. Love never fails.

5

The Intentions of God

For whom he did foreknow, he also did predestinate to be conformed to the image of his Son, that he might be the firstborn among many brethren.

Romans 8:29, KJV

Some people spend their entire Christian lives wondering about the purpose of their existence. Out of duty or social pressure, they never miss a church service or religious event. Yet in the back of their minds is the nagging thought that there has to be something more to spiritual life than this, and they are right! If duty and pressure are the only motivation, then God's desire for us has been missed. God did not create us so we could be religious. He didn't create us so we could go to the "right" church. Almighty God created us so we might be a pleasure to Him. God is not satisfied so long as there are unregenerate people in the world. Many unregenerate people are outside the church, but many are inside, too. These are the people who say they carry His name yet have no impact on society at large. If our beliefs do not express themselves in the society where people are, it is empty religion. Nothing drives people farther or faster from the heart of God than empty religion.

God owns the earth, created the earth, and is accountable only to Himself for what it becomes. He has no intention of waiting until every vestige of His character has been lost from the earth before He acts. This is why Jesus Christ came to earth and initiated the process of reconciling us to God.

Everything we are about centers around the intentions of God. In God's time every aspect of His plan will be in full operation. Right now we have a choice, but the day of judgment is fast approaching. If, on that day, there is an ocean of souls who have set their face against God, God will not have failed. They chose not to respond. Whether or not we choose to be part of God's plan, His intentions will become reality.

Some people come to Christ through their own search or a Damascus Road experience. The vast majority of us, however, come to Christ because of people who have had an impact on our lives. We become the fruit or spiritual offspring of their lives. Today, after two thousand years of spiritual birth and rebirth, we have more knowledge, the completed Scriptures, and more material blessing than all the generations preceding us. Why is it then, that fewer and fewer people are coming to Christ?

In his letter to Timothy, Paul said that he preached the gospel to the whole world. Now instead of progressing, we have regressed. In Paul's day they didn't have the completed Bible. Paul had studied the major and minor prophets and the first five books of the Old Testament. Only the educated, such as the Pharisees, had read them and passed them down. For the first few centuries there was nothing written down. Everything was passed to the next generation by word of mouth.

Ezra read the Scripture to the people all day long, and they broke out in praise and worship to God, grateful that they could hear the Word and the scribes could give them an understanding of the Scripture.

We not only want to be changed to become people who have a heart tender enough to receive His truths, but we want to be the expression of God that centers around our being in His like-ness. It began with the Word, the revelation of God to man. God is no different than His Word. "In the beginning was the Word, and the Word was with God, and the Word was God" (John 1:1). In Him is life and there is no darkness at all. Jesus came to give us life. His words impart life. God's intention toward us is that, first of all, we become partakers of the life now available through Christ's death and resurrection. When we find the free-dom that is in Christ, we become active participants in God's plan to fill the earth once again with His image—deity to humanity, with humanity bearing the image of deity.

God wants to change our nature and build upon that. That is the bottom line as it relates to Christianity. What we do is the fruit of who we are. The same is true of God. You can find out who God is by looking at what He does. In the beginning God created others to bear His image. This is exactly what He expects us to do. He wants us to birth spiritual offspring to bear His image.

The fact that the Spirit of God dwells inside us does not sug-gest that He isn't invisible and eternal. It simply means that He, who is formless, chose to reside inside our form. What form is character? What form is love? What form is meekness? What form is kindness? Of course, our physical form doesn't matter. God wants to change our nature. God is calling us back to who He is, the infinite character of His nature that is not confined or defined.

When you are in a state of unbelief, you make the infinite God finite in your life. Unbelief says that there is something facing you that God can't handle. By our unbelief we strip our-selves of the potential to experience the power of God and ful-fill His intentions. His work will still go forward, He'll just have to find somebody else to do it. Unbelief doesn't change God, but it does prevent us from becoming His channel of blessing and power to others. God expresses His intentions through people who will not isolate themselves from His agenda by their unbelief. God is never confined. Inside you, He will be everything that He is if you will only have faith.

Atoms are invisible but express great power under certain conditions. While this is a finite example, it could be a way to think about the power of God in our lives. Is there a lack of God's power in your life? Just because He is not expressing Himself now, or you don't see it now, does not mean He is limited. He may not agree with your request. He may be testing you, or you may be limiting His access to your heart because of your unbelief.

God's power will come in God's way, in God's time, and for God's purposes. We must not expect His power to fit into our preconceived, rational notion of what it has to be. God often takes us out of the whole dimension of rationality.

Maturity Allows God to Compromise Our Plans

By the spoken word of God we understand worlds were made. Whenever we start making something, we begin by gathering materials. God doesn't need anything. He already has it. When we launch out to do something, nothing is impossible to us if what we are doing is of God. While we live under the power of the Almighty, that power is available to fulfill His purposes. His purposes are not always our purposes however. Maturity allows God to compromise our plans without a reaction that questions His goodness to us.

It is time to recognize that it is God who is at work, not you. You are merely God's servant to fulfill His intentions. If you are faithful to your plans rather than the plan of God, you are setting yourself up for a major setback. You can do nothing of eternal value in your own strength. Every Christian must let go of the idea that God's activity in our lives has to fit into our understanding of how things should be. God is not and will not be confined to our understand of how He should act. The Bible is very clear on this point. How can the clay say to the potter, "Why have you made me like this?" Make a decision to stop questioning God's activity in your life. No matter what your circumstances, your entire perspective will change if you recognize the truth that God is at work in your life. Consider Paul and Silas in prison, or Stephen as he was being stoned, or any of history's martyrs as they kept their eyes on Christ while suffering. These circumstances often seem senseless from a human standpoint. But never forget, God is the God of history and He is following through on His intentions in your life and in the world.

It is relatively easy to accept God's refining activity in someone else's life. People go through hardship, and we are quick to recognize the hand of God in their lives. Isn't it odd that our keen spiritual perception becomes dulled so quickly when God includes us in that refining process? When difficulties come, no longer is it an opportunity to remain faithful to God regardless of the strain. At such times, Satan gets all the attention as we turn our opportunity for praise to God into a fight with the devil, so sure are we that God would never do anything but shower us with material blessings and perfect health.

When God created man in His image, He then breathed the breath of life into him and man became a living soul. Before God did that, what was man? A lump of clay! Can clay speak? Yes, but only after God breathes into it, giving it life. Can His creation ask why it was made or how it is being used? We have been created by God. You and I must accept that we are clay in the hands of an almighty God.

All this deals with pride. We all need worm training. God cannot trust us if we are constantly second-guessing Him. How can He give us understanding at a time when we are still asking questions relating to our creation and why things are allowed to happen? It is okay to ask questions, but questioning God should be done in holy fear. The potter can deface the clay. He can crush it all the way down and build it up again. We are clay and have been made to talk. We cannot comprehend Him who made us, we cannot understand Him unless He grants us that understanding. So if we are to ask a question, it is to be asked in the utmost humility.

There are levels of worm training we need that are not found in the thoughts of Americans. We have many major universities. I was surprised to learn that the Puritans founded Harvard because they thought we needed a training school for creating men of God. Now the students hardly know their historical roots, and if they do, they look upon those early Puritans condescendingly. With an attitude of pride, they consider the Puritans ignorant and superstitious. What they don't realize is that it is they who have gotten dumber because they know less about their purpose. Even if they knew about their purpose, having gotten further from it only shows their ignorance, not their intellect. They have become so blind they think they are more intelligent. Their dumbness came because they have moved further away from the creative purpose of the university itself, let alone going back to the creative order of the creation of man. Without humility it is presumptuous to think that you can even have a university that will train you and teach you something about God. God's intentions will come to fruition regardless of who ignores or rebels against Him. Haughty Harvard has chosen to sit on the sidelines of God's game plan.

Jesus says no man can know the Son except the Father reveals Him. The presumption of many early universities was to teach students to know God. But God doesn't reveal Himself just because we build a building. You can have a university (or a church, for that matter) and learn a lot of facts about God and still not know God. Knowing God is totally the prerogative of God Himself. If God does not reveal Himself, you can know about God and never know Him, just like we can know about people and never personally know them. We can read books about them, study them, even meet them, and still not know them. There are literary scholars on every ancient personality who think we really understand how these men thought and who they were by what we read about them. Yet all we know is what has been written down.

Have you ever thought you knew someone for years then discovered you did not really know them? Not only were you not interpreting them correctly, but they did not give you an accurate picture of themselves. If all we know is what someone else writes, how can we know the true inner nature? You can see how far we could be from knowing anything, much less knowing God. I am dealing with the matter of worm training. Who do we think we are that we could be anything less than absolutely broken? We are but clay in the hands of a potter.

The arrogance of questioning God is demonstrated by not knowing who you are, because you cannot know who you are until you know the one who made you. You cannot know the one who made you unless He reveals Himself to you, regardless of how much you may know about Him.

God spends more time seeking us than we spend getting to know Him. This also shows His nature. How undeserving we are. That in itself should break us. Why would a holy God who created the clay make man from that clay and then desire fellowship with him? Because He sees you for the potential He has placed in you. He knows you are not there yet, but He has taken His nature and brought you to the place where in His plan you are worthy. You cannot get there alone. God has to bring you.

I really want to please the Lord, but how can I unless He helps me? How can I ever be boastful or prideful when I am at peace, knowing I was brought there by His mercy and grace.

Have mercy upon me, O God, according to thy lovingkindness: according unto the multitude of thy tender mercies blot out my transgressions.

Psalm 51:1, KJV

This was written after David had sinned with Bathsheba, Solomon's mother. The heir to the kingdom of David was a child of his sin. The fact that God allowed the heir to inherit the throne shows that man on his own could never deserve or earn such results on his merit. We are heirs through the mercy of God, just like King Solomon. We often chaff at this kind of divine selection when we see it in other's lives. Amazing that our holy God is more merciful than we are. But God doesn't do things man's way. God says, "My thoughts are not your thoughts, nor are your ways my ways" (Isa. 55:8).

There is a divine agitation inside me when I consider that my thoughts may not be God's thoughts and my ways may not be God's ways. They may come from the devil. I have been wonderfully and fearfully made. I fear and reverence God so He can impart to me a new awareness and intensity for being like Him and with the right spirit. Psalm 55 deals with that. Look at the heart of David. God said he was a man after His own heart. He followed God's intentions.

When We Turn Our Trauma over to God It Becomes Training

This is why God is working in us as a church. It is heart surgery, and surgery of this kind always leaves scar tissue. The scar says

God has operated on us. As you look back at hurts you have sustained, there are scars from life's experiences. The operation of God brought you here. God could have let you be destroyed. But no. You are part of His redemptive plan for the world. He has sought you out with your background and every traumatic experience in your life. It is proof of God's grace to bring you where you should be. When we turn our trauma over to God, it becomes training for His purposes. We have to come to this. Listen to me as a worm.

The potter sets the clay where he will. Repent of wishing to be something other than what God made you to be. Male, female, rich, poor, black, or white; don't ever want to be anything different because God, the potter, chose how the clay was going to be formed, and you are wonderfully and beautifully made. You do not have the prerogative to make such wishes because it assumes you know what is better for you than your creator, the potter. Your journey is to find out what God wants to do with you as His clay and to realize that you are greatly valued. God never creates objects that have no value.

The potter can set you where He wants to set you. He can allow circumstances to happen in your life or prevent them. It makes no difference, you are His vessel for honor or dishonor. Get out of your mind the thought that greatness deals with the size of a ministry. Greatness deals with the ability that God gives you to handle trouble. Do not reproach His nature in your assessment of what you have gone through. Greatness does not consist in reducing others to your service, but reducing yourself to their's.

You find keys to worshiping Him in what you have gone through. Therefore provoke darkness, showing God's shining light in the midst of darkness. That is when light shines the brightest. We have been taught that once we are saved then God will prevent us from having to endure anything unpleasant.

This is a lie of the devil to cause us to feel disappointment with God. On the contrary, He instead qualifies us to go through the trials. When we endure tribulations, we automatically ask why. We should be asking if there is anything God wants to teach that we are not seeing. In asking that kind of question, we open ourselves to receive God's intentions for us.

It Is More Important to Obey Than to Understand

Some questions are asked out of a lack of understanding, others demonstrate a supreme lack of humility. At times we don't know our place before God. It is hard to remember that you are a piece of clay in the potter's hand. When our questions come from sincere anguish of spirit, the Gentle Shepherd has mercy: "My God, my God, why have You forsaken Me? . . . I am a worm, and no man" (Ps. 22:1, 6). This means, "I am just a worm. Do with me what You want. I do not deserve to know." It is more important that you obey than that you understand. Job revealed the depth of His commitment to God when he said, "Though He slay me, yet will I serve Him." Was that necessarily the right assessment of what was really happening from God's perspective? No. But it was the right conclusion.

What is the truth? You cannot serve Him unless He gives you the strength to serve Him. What is the revelation? We are the fruit of His labor, the product of His intentions.

Lord, help me not to resist getting whatever glory out of me that you have chosen. Do not let me have a wrong assessment of what you intend—nor a wrong attitude. Help me be full of grace in the midst of trouble.

You can't get into the military unless you are in good physical shape. You can't run track unless you're fit. You can't play basketball unless you hone your skills. How do you expect to be an effective, useful part of God's intention for mankind until you get in the shape He intends you to be in? Getting into shape is a process of practice, testing, and pushing through the hard times until you get to the end of yourself. If you cannot pass the level where you are, you will certainly never reach the next level. You have to spend yourself to gain ground.

This is how God is calling you to prepare to be a participant in His plan. You submit and you die to all your priorities and your schedule. You may never receive anything back in this life. But "Eye hath not seen, nor ear heard, of the glory prepared for them that love Him" (1 Cor. 2:9). Your reward, like Stephen's, may be in the world to come.

Don't pay any attention to your impulses to get your own ministry or get into the limelight. That is not what you should be after. All that is up to God. It is more of a challenge to work in humility and brokenness in the position of leadership than the position you are in right now. You are in a position to get more rewards than I am right now. You are largely unknown. You are not getting credit for anything now. Once you become a leader, everybody gives you credit, and if God does not humble you, you would steal Jesus' reward and get all of yours on earth. You have to have the grace of God not to take it, and it isn't easy.

I stand up to speak saying, "I give God the glory," but God holds the reins. He knows whether or not I like it, whether I want more of Him or more of the spotlight. Sometimes He gives me a clearer glimpse of myself. Lately, I have recognized by the grace of God that I like attention. That isn't me saying that, it is the Lord. There is something about leadership that relates to charisma and self-exaltation. It is such a thin line. Only God knows the difference between humility and self-promotion. Lately, He has been asking me to examine myself.

In selecting the conferences where I would speak at Promise Keepers, I chose the ones I believed the Lord wanted me at, and a funny thing happened—the ones I chose ended up being the smallest ones. I didn't choose the smallest ones, God chose them for me. In my mind I was thinking, "They need this anointing God is giving me. I have a new spirit. They need this humility. They need my prayer life." The Lord showed me that is absolutely not why I was there. He said, "You esteem yourself more highly than you ought to. You are not a worm. You talk about being a worm, but you are not one. I have proven you." What can I say except, "I am sorry, Lord. Please have mercy on me and forgive me"?

As the stakes get higher and the opportunities greater, I want them. It is the slickness of the devil that I can come up with numerous spiritual reasons in justification. But God is working in my heart. I am focusing on being uncompromising in my message. I am working with leaders rather than going after the numbers. I know all of this, so I must be humble. It is so easy to be deceived when you are in a position of leadership. God could have let me go on in that deception. After a while, if enough people tell you the Lord is raising you up for this hour, it is easy to really begin to like that, even unconsciously.

A businessman approached me in Fort Worth and told me how he had been impacted by my ministry at Promise Keepers a couple of years previous. During our conversation about people he knew and things that happened, the Lord began to speak to me through this man. He said I should not worry about the number of places where I go as a minister because if the numbers were there I would get a wrong estimation of what God was doing. The fact that not many people show up proves that there is a need. The man told me I should learn how to just show up and stop advertising. This hit me strongly. How much substance do you have? What can you build by just showing up?

We can trace the journeys of Jesus and Paul after they went out into evangelism, but many of the people in those towns had no notice that they were coming. They just showed up and God did something after they got there. What does that do to my advertising campaign? He didn't say I should not advertise. God does not want me to follow along the popular ministries and ministers' style of self-promotion. In Jesus' ministry He chose relatively few to serve closely with Him. The closer you were in His inner circle, the stronger you were rebuked. Think of how many people enjoyed serving from afar when they saw how He dealt with the Pharisees, scribes, and Sadducees!

We Want to Hide Our Number-One Asset—Inadequacy

Even though I am way down, think how many people are not close to me because they don't want to be exposed; they cannot handle the rebuke. Others are not close because they do not want to be seen. We want to hide our inadequacies when that is our number-one asset. People who were the closest to Jesus were the people who felt they had the greatest need. You let the people who think they have something to offer be the ones to draw closer to the ones who have the giftings. Jesus says those who need much or have been given much, love much.

The most intense people are those with the greatest needs. You need the greatest impartation. Your deception is that you have more talent then you need. I ask God to help me never to put confidence in my own speaking ability. The devil tries his best to trick me when I am complimented on something I have said. I know most people are being kind. I still have trouble conjugating verbs. I am familiar with correct grammar, but when I start preaching I don't try to remember the rules. The

Lord makes me insecure even about my language. I find myself trying to be proper. That is pride. It is not natural to me. Learn to do it naturally and quit trying to impress people. People are hearing something from the heart of God. It can come out of ignorant, unlearned people like Peter, John, and James—fishermen. The gospel they preached and the character of Christ that radiated from them caused people to marvel that they had been with Jesus.

You've Got to Prepare for the Game

Every serious ball player has to prepare before the game. If you do not prepare, you will not have what it takes when crunch time comes around. You have to be in shape. We are in a season where we are getting in shape. The fourth quarter is coming. When you look at all the things like wars, rumors of war, and earthquakes, all those things don't deal with you physically. It deals with you inwardly. You will never know if a man will break under pressure until he finds himself in a pressure situation.

If, in the game of golf, I do not practice difficult shots and troublesome situations, then at some pressure time I will not be able to handle it. "In much tribulation shall you enter into the kingdom of God." Tribulation means pressure. We have been taught a theology of avoiding pressure rather than embracing it. We have been taught to be soft. In training and preparing ourselves, we should be teaching strength in adversity through the power of God.

God works brokenness in you before you can finish growing up. He is making us profitable in His sight. Whenever we receive exaltation, it is secondary. What God is doing has much more substance than that. Have His intentions for you taken you down a difficult road? Keep your eyes on Him. He is teaching you how to be crushed, to be ignored and moved aside for His greater glory.

Before a Worm Is Used as Bait
It Has to be Put on a Hook

This is what happens to the worm. Its primary use is to aerate the earth and catch fish. Before they are used as bait they have to be put on a hook. Jesus is hooking you. Let Him do it. You are the bait. God throws you out into the deep. You are out there to catch fish. There is an attractiveness to you for God's purpose. Jesus says, "He that eateth me shall live by me" (John 6:57). You may have been feeding people something you are not living by. You can become the worm that God uses to catch the fish.

God put me on His hook and I cannot get off. He put me on but will readily take me off if I become ineffective. Help me, Lord, to remain on the hook so I can catch souls for the kingdom and play my part in Your intention to fill the earth with your image.

6

Can Jesus Count on You?

Then said I, Lo, I come: in the volume of the book it is written of me, I delight to do thy will, O my God: yea, thy law is within my heart.

Psalm 40:7–8, KJV

Not long ago I was holding a series of meetings in the Dallas–Fort Worth area. There was a couple, new in the Lord, who faithfully came to the seminars. When we had occasion to meet some time after the event, they shared their growing concern and conviction about a statement I often make: Our present stewardship will determine our future responsibility.

Hungry for God and His Word, they sought substantive teaching and prayed for understanding. As with many committed Christian parents, this couple was also concerned about raising their three sons to be champions for the Lord. They were all too mindful of the sin-sick world in which they had to raise their children, a world that is designed to corrupt them.

It is impossible to open a newspaper, turn on the radio, or watch television news and avoid hearing about the rise of violence and lawlessness in our land. As we spoke, this couple shared their deep compassion for the three-year-old child dead at the hands of a Los Angeles gang when the car in which she was riding was riddled by gunfire after making a wrong turn down a cul-de-sac. They pondered what prompted Susan

Smith to buckle her two young sons into the backseat of her car and let them tragically drown. Where was God? Could they trust Him? Couldn't He do something about these tragedies?

Then, as if God touched their minds with the clarity of truth, the answer to their sincere questioning came. The husband stood up and with a look of one given a precious gift he said, "This discussion has nothing to do with if we can trust Him. The issue is, can He count on us?"

The Issue Is: Can He Count on Us?

Eliminating God from our thinking and lives is the precursor to ruin. Moses, while preparing Israel for nationhood, warned against ignoring God. The pages of the Bible are filled with the consequences of ignoring God. With only lip service, many people say they trust Jesus. These are meaningless words if Jesus cannot trust you. Either Jesus is Lord of all or He is not Lord at all.

The seeking couple joined a growing force of believers who want to move to higher levels of walking with Christ. They passionately want a breakthrough from heaven to catch a vision of where they are going spiritually and how to take future generations with them.

These searching souls are significant to my ministry. They are hungry. They are willing to pay the price of commitment— and there is a price. I find blessing in working with them and leading them back, back, back into the Scripture. Together we search out the question, Where are we going in this transitory life? Those who are serious enough to submit themselves to God's calling in their lives, allowing God to count on them, receive an understanding of God's intention to fill the earth with His image through generational transfer as modeled in His Word.

In earlier pages we touched on the Lord saying, "I am the God of Abraham, Isaac, and Jacob." Each of these patriarchs represented a generation and transferred two things. These men experienced a visitation from God. They also possessed natural wealth. Both were transferable.

In this generation we emphasize more of what we need naturally than what we are called by God to transfer spiritually. Watch this! Where does God say we are going? From glory to glory, faith to faith, grace to grace, and strength to strength.

This is what Abraham passed down to Isaac. He was to become the heir to the substance of his father's revelation. Then from his own personal devotion, Isaac added more substance, and it grew exponentially. He passed his faithfulness down, literally becoming an exponent of the principles of God to his own son.

Isaac received the revelation from his father, spent his own life receiving from God, and poured his combined revelation into his son, Jacob. We see the generational progression in the faith of patriarchs. God has no grandchildren, but faithful fathers can model the knowledge and character of Christ to their children, spiritual and natural. When the revelation of Christ is faithfully passed down from generation to generation, the outcome is destined to increase! Christianity was meant to be self-propagating. The psalmist wrote, "One generation shall praise thy works to another, and shall declare thy mighty acts" (Ps. 145:4). Isaiah indicated the fruit of godly legacy for future generations: "I will pour out My Spirit on your offspring, and My blessing on your descendants; . . . The living, the living, he shall praise thee, as I do this day: the father to the children shall make known thy truth" (Isa. 44:3, NASB; Isa. 38:19, KJV).

For too long, Christian men in America have overlooked and ignored this generational imperative. This is not an option or a recommendation. It is our duty before almighty God and is for our benefit. Can Jesus count on you in this matter?

Let's move back further to some rare truth that strikes me even as I write. It occurs to me that when we look at Adam in terms of what God created him to be—being made in the image and likeness of God—authority comes into focus. God gave Adam unequivocal authority over the fish, birds, and things that creep on the earth. Yet with all that authority, he was to reside inside an opulent garden. He was to remain there and care for it.

Our Present Stewardship Will Determine Our Future Responsibility

This is a message that we desperately need to understand. Adam was given authority over the creations of the earth, from the large to the small, but God's plan for Adam was to begin from the small and work toward the large. His garden cultivation began with one area of stewardship. As Adam was faithful in bearing the image of God in the garden, God's image would naturally spread over the face of the earth as Adam's seed continued to have dominion. This is one example of how God considers our present stewardship to determine our future responsibility.

Had there been no sin, it is obvious where Adam was heading: into the magnitude of eternal responsibility. Generational faithfulness, passed down to the sons, begets the same. Without sin, Adam would still be alive and very much in control.

When Adam was tempted, he failed. Jesus was the antithesis, for when He was tempted, He succeeded. It does not take a theologian to recognize where Adam would have gone with his original authority. Jesus, the last Adam, through obedience, fulfilled all of His father's intentions.

When a person is saved, he starts down the road of biblical progression, the road to maturity. Think of it as the principle of gradualism. When God calls upon us to conform to His image in a small matter, we have a choice. If we yield to temptation, we lose ground and demonstrate that we are not yielded to God. If we resist the devil and choose for God, we demonstrate to God that we are ready for greater responsibility. Such trials become the test for character development and qualifies or disqualifies us for greater realms of kingdom authority.

The Dallas couple are seeing and developing from the small to the large. They have become a family determined to walk with kingdom vision and reign in righteousness demonstrated in their developing earthly stewardship. Generational progression has begun. Truth is being processed and passed on to their children, so their spiritual breakthroughs will be early and significant. Training children in the way they should go by living example, the fruit of such effort will then be passed on in future generations.

This life is preparation for what agape love requires—giving. Will we be judged as to whether or not Jesus could trust us? Don't ever doubt it. This is the reason for the judgment seat of Christ. At that time He will delegate to the body of Christ, heirs of the inheritance of substance, practical jurisdictional authority over creative works according to their faithfulness. If we till with diligence our patch of His work, progressively we move toward higher levels of responsibility.

Are You with Me?

These truths are presented in Daniel 7 where the Ancient of Days gives the kingdom to the Son. The Son, it says, shall take the kingdom and give it to the saints, and the saints shall possess the kingdom forever and forever. It is important not to miss the fact that the kingdom represents all of creation. Many will ask, "Will our dominion in eternity just build the earth?" Of course not. We have to look at where Jesus' authority is. It is in the heavens. Don't shout me down now! I believe there will be interplanetary travel. There will be people in authority in the uttermost parts of creation. Those in authority will have been faithful from the small to the large, their responsibility directly commensurate with the level of spiritual development they reached here on earth. What a challenge to those who are mature enough to look out into the distances of God and see what He sees. How tragic a vast number of Christians sacrifice their future on the altar of their immediate earthly desires. These truths are not the meanderings of Wellington Boone. They come airmail from God and His spirit through the Word, directed to serious Christians.

Often I am asked why God's saints have to suffer in the process of preparing to rule and reign with Him. Remind yourself, God looks from His viewpoint and sees what He is forming in us. If the saints in honesty search for meaning in tribulation and emerge without rebellion, they are moving forward. He does not leave us orphans in testing and trial. He is with us and seeks to work out His will in our lives during times of discomfort. He is the Father, the Sovereign, the almighty God. Fathers have the right to rule as they best see fit for their children. We know that a good, earthly father adores his own, wanting the very best for them. How much more our heavenly Father will perfect that which is His own. Father God always has in His mind what is best from the perspective of eternity. From earth we only see the minuteness of present suffering. As the Puritans would say, "We live and move in Christ, often without explanation, but God is the only explanation we need. His disciplines are for our perfection so that we may share His holiness. Our diminishment is part of the journey toward perfection." If we are to become part of His destiny, we are called upon to share His death and sufferings, because though He was a son, He learned obedience by the things that He suffered.

We Aren't Defined by What We Are Going Through but by How We Go Through It

Is it unnatural to be bold to question God? Job did. What better time than now to learn the principle of suffering and loss as a higher dimension moving you, in the Spirit, toward spiritual gain? It is the beginning of being better formed in His image. There is a reason why we are not defined by what we are going through but how we go through it. Why? Because how we go through something is the basis upon our standing in the next world. It bears testimony to the degree to which we have conformed to the character of Christ Jesus.

When He was reviled, He reviled not again. They spat upon Him and whipped Him, they pressed razor-sharp thorns into His head. Notice this. He still stayed true to the nature of the worm as expressed in Psalm 22. In that context, He met the approval of a just God and followed in the character of God, further accepting God's mandate that He go all the way to Golgotha.

Jesus would not be distracted by the crowd or the press of people. He became a faithful succorer, the person who brings relief, going to the aid of the distressed. He also profiled the obedient servant so we would have a clear, perfect role model to follow.

Observing the church today, most look to Him for what He can do for them. They seek His miracles and signs and look for wonders. Few choose to follow the part of servanthood and obedience. Jesus does not appear to be surprised by that common reaction, because in Luke He asks who is greater, he who sits at the table or he who serves? His answer, "Is it not he who sits at the table? Yet I am among you as the One who serves" (Luke 22:27). He set forth the example without question.

This passage is amazing. He continued,

> But you are those who have continued with Me in My trials. And I bestow upon you a kingdom, just as My Father bestowed one upon Me, that you may eat and drink at My table in My kingdom and on thrones judging the twelve tribes of Israel.
>
> *Luke* 22:28–30

What an incredible statement in mediating competition that had arisen among the disciples. Who would sit at His right hand? Who on the left? Which one of these guys gets the seat at the head table, the box seats at the ball game, or star status at a public event? They had it all wrong.

The discussion of who would eat and drink at His table was not a discussion of food or drink, but the substance it would take to handle the jurisdiction that He was going to give to them. We are assured of this by His words in John 5. His "meat" was to do the will of God and finish His work. Literally, He was eating the substance of the revelation.

> Then said I, Lo, I come: in the volume of the book it is written of me, I delight to do thy will, O my God: yea, thy law is within my heart.
>
> *Psalm* 40:7–8, KJV

Indeed He was partaking of the good of the revelation of the intentions of the Father. That was His motivation for eating physical food. Take away the will of God from Him, and He had no reason to eat physical food. Why? Because He would be ready to die. Deuteronomy 8 revealed man shall not live by bread alone but by every word that proceeds out of the mouth of God. That is the purest of natural food, revolutionary eating from the substance of who He is, the substance of the intentions of God for our lives. Therein is the source of equal opportunity! Jeremiah underlined the truth by saying,

> Your words were found, and I ate them, And Your word was to me the joy and rejoicing of my heart; For I am called by Your name, O LORD God of hosts.
>
> *Jeremiah* 15:16

It is important for us to delineate who sits at the table in His kingdom and therefore sits on the thrones, judging the twelve tribes of Israel. Many in the ministry explain the judgment seat of Christ as a place where they look for crowns. When asked what will be the reward for which the crowns are offered, most don't have a clue.

We must go back again to see Jesus being called the last Adam. When Adam failed, he lost the essence of what God created him for, which was to procreate and to rule. In this case, rule the family. Jesus rules over His family. He does not inherit only physical, geographical creation. He inherits people. Taking people away from creation has no value. Ultimately when the Lord says, "You're going to sit on kingdoms," He means that you are going to have jurisdictional authority over people. That is why we grow in the character of God, so we will qualify to handle His kind of responsibility.

This is rare truth because you look at both creation and Adam. Then consider Abraham, Isaac, Jacob, and Joseph. Include Daniel. All of these men had authority over people. If we break this down to our governmental structures today, we have mayors, governors, CEOs, and presidents. These are authority figures. The model exists today. The difference is we will be doing it with perfect character in eternity. What a contrast to the present day.

"The heaven, even the heavens, are the Lord's: but the earth hath he given to the children of men" (Ps. 115:16, KJV). It is revealing to some that the Bible singles out the earth as being of importance in the scheme of things in this immense universe. Contrast earth to the heavens. It is but a tiny, insignificant speck. But it was on earth that God created man in His image and to earth that He sent His Son to be savior. It is to earth He will return, but the reign is universal.

The determining factor of the rewards we receive will be dependent on what we allow the Holy Spirit to work in us of His nature. God chooses who would be one with Him. Preeminence is determined by His choice. That is what sovereignty is all about, even down to who is going to be born first. In the Old Testament and in many cultures still today, the firstborn male son bears the privilege and responsibility to rule. So the Lord then decides who is the elder son, and he gets rewarded based upon the decision of God. Remember, we are not judged by our position but by our faithfulness in whatever position we happen to be in.

In terms of faithfulness, we are given individual choice even as Jesus was confronted with choice. There is the potential that, even though the firstborn male should be the heir of the father, in this case, Jesus, as the only begotten, is the heir of all things. He is not just the heir by created order, He is the heir by faithfulness to the will of the Father. As the son of man, He earned the inheritance.

In this matter of rewards, we do not forget that salvation is justification by grace through faith alone. However, rewards are earned. Consider this. He alone has to judge. In 1 Corinthians 5:3 and 2 Corinthians 3:11—5:10, He informs us that He will see to it what sort of rewards are conferred. Gold, silver, precious stones, wood, hay, or stubble are written in His ledger and will be called to stand the test of fire.

Today we find it tempting to equate rewards with the results of large, visible ministries. But the determining factor, before God, is not the work that we do but the work that we allow the Holy Spirit to do in our hearts.

Jesus is the Joshua of the New Testament. Joshua is the Jesus of the Old Testament. One was outside, the other was inside. The greater the Lord works into us the substance of His reality, the longer our work for Him endures. What is from within has weight to it, resembling the weight of the glory that the high priests had when they were to face the Red Sea. The weight of the glory of the ark that they carried left an imprint in the sand. Remember? That imprint had to do with the substance of God in us for the generations that would follow.

How full is the church with lightweight Christians who do not let the glory and substance of God work within them. It all comes back to priorities and whether or not God can count on you. God demands allegiance and being in charge. Jesus said his Father decides which of us will sit on the right or the left. Interpreted, it means placement will mirror different levels of spiritual proximity to Him. This is the Bible. This is God's distinct plan that is in motion today, tomorrow, and until it is fulfilled in His kingdom.

I like to go even further because Jesus goes further. Looking at the first three chapters of Genesis and the last three chapters of Revelation, you find the beginning and the fulfillment of the beginning. It is set forth and in motion. You will notice things there that relate to Adam being placed in the garden. Jesus obtained victory in the garden. The tree of life in Genesis comes from the spring of God in Revelation. It is stunning to compare these differences and discover Jesus fulfills something that began in Adam.

How He started is the way He ended. How is this accomplished? By asking God to open our eyes and let us see. Then the eyes of our understanding are enlightened, and we know where we are ultimately going by looking at how it all started in the beginning. Nothing has changed. God does not change His mind as the wind blows. His will and word are forever sealed in heaven. God has adjusted to man's inadequacy in the process, but it surely must grieve Him. He has not lowered His standard, He is headed the same way. He is still building His church. Can He count on you?

It is fascinating that we can observe that Israel is being called, but at the same time not being chosen. Some would describe this as being in the outer court of the tabernacle. It is said that you are Israel, but you are in the outer court. Who really wants to be on the outside? Yet this is clear in the Bible. It becomes relevant when you say, the outer court sun by day and moon by night. That represents being carnal and is at a sense-level of knowledge. In the holy place, you have the light of the seven-branch candlestick. When you come there you have gone through the mixing and kneading of the bread, being put in shape, in the oven of testing and burning that signifies being broken.

You sit at that golden table and wait for the priest to come in to offer incense on the golden altar. There is no natural light inside. That takes a different level of commitment. It also takes a different quality of life. The people could not go in the holy place; only the priests could enter. Once they got past the brazen altar they went to the brazen laver to wash and change clothes. It is intuitively understood that the closer you get to the Lord, the more your life has to be transformed. Washed, purified, and made ready by the washing and regeneration of the Word and the renewing of the Holy Ghost. This is the focus of an obedient lifestyle. If these priests missed one point of the law, they were history—dead. The rules of the tabernacle were irrevocable. Those leaders did not fool around with inappropriate behavior or careless worship. It was ultra-serious.

Today we are safe behind grace, yet cheap grace does not please God. Too many have the impression that grace means God will let wrongs done with purpose pass without consequence. That is a misinterpretation, because under grace the expectation of heaven says I am more willing to be obedient to the law. The difference is, as I have written before, the law comes not from the outside. I allow the law to work in my heart. So now the people of God should be willing, in experiencing the reality of God, to not only do the Word, but allow the Word to become synonymous with their being. Christ in me the hope of glory.

God is after people who accept the unmerited favor of grace to walk in obedience to His will. Again, preparation for "marrying" Jesus. That represents union of spirit, soul, and body. The marriage model can misrepresent this. For Christ it has to be a marriage into His ways, His mind, His life, His spirit. This is so that you become one in Him.

In 1 Thessalonians 5:23 (KJV), Paul prayed: "I pray God your whole spirit and soul and body be preserved blameless." This represents man as a threefold being. He is spirit, clarified in 1 Corinthians 6:17 that he has joined unto the Lord and has one spirit with Him. He has a soul. That is the emotional aspect of a life, and he has will. "For the word of God is living and powerful and sharper than any two-edged sword, piercing even to the division of soul and spirit, and of joints and marrow, and is a discerner of the thoughts and intents of the heart" (Heb. 4:12).

Spirit, soul, and body given over to God for His purposes is a worthy aim but also reasonable service. Preparation for reigning in all eternity takes guts and guidance. Why are we so caught up in the moment instead of making every moment count as training for eternity?

The young couple from Dallas are committed to making a difference in their home, through their home and outside of their home. With united spirit, souls, and bodies, they have been moving. Some obstacles that confront them seem insurmountable, but they keep on keeping on because the love of Christ constrains them. "Because we judge thus: that if One died for all, then all died; and He died for all, that those who live should live no longer for themselves, but for Him who died for them and rose again" (2 Cor. 5:14–15). When resurrection power kicks in, power is unleashed and obstacles overcome. A carefully created calligraphic hangs on the inside of their front door. It reads: Can Jesus count on you today?

Their intensity is reminiscent of a hero of the faith who knew obstacles, faced them, and though little known in evangelical circles today, he is well known in heaven.

William Wilberforce was born to privilege more than two centuries ago. He walked among the nobles and princes of England. He often was the prized guest at high teas and political events. Some referred to him as the wittiest man on the Continent.

He had grown up in the church. He took on the cloak of being a Christian, but it was for outward appearance rather than being changed from within. Because of his oratorical skills, he did well at Cambridge University. At the age of twenty-one he ran for Parliament. He began as a dark horse, but his skill and rhetoric brought him the election and a seat in the House of Commons. A seat he retained for forty-five years.

In the summer four years later his mother asked him to accompany her on a trip to Switzerland. An old friend, trusted schoolmaster Isaac Milner, was invited to join them. Milner was a scholar and a jovial individual. The two made a great traveling team, spending hours discussing life, Parliament, and the teachings of Christ. Milner was a genuine Christian.

While steaming toward France, Milner suggested that Wilberforce read a classic of Philip Doddridge, *The Rise and Progress of Religion*. Assuming it would help him in Parliament, Wilberforce spent time deep in the book.

Struck by the example of Milner and a new understanding of the meaning of the atonement of Christ, Wilberforce launched his quest toward spiritual things as the ship docked. However, after returning to Parliament, he fell back into the former circle of friends and kept God at arm's length.

Meanwhile, the Doddridge message was percolating in his soul, and he turned to his friend Milner once again. Traveling together, they read the Greek New Testament. As they did, the spirit of God drove His words into Wilberforce's inner life, transforming him. Immediately the Word became food and drink, and he is said to have often missed meals while studying the Old Testament.

The Word found good soil in this parliamentarian's life much like the young couple in Dallas two centuries later. Wilberforce was determined to change his ways and live "as unto God and to exchange the past weakness into God's strength" and discover "what God intendeth for me to do, not just now but in the forever."

Family and friends were convinced Wilberforce had gone mad. In the upper classes of England, a sincere Christian was scarce. The Wesleyan revival had moved across the poor and wretched but missed those who were secure in themselves. To the amazement of his friends, Wilberforce became more endearing to them as he modeled Christ and was "living sober and kind, displaying a new compassion and was more reasonable and assured. England should take note."

Struggling with his destiny, he wondered if he should resign and seek something more of God. He was led to John Newton, as different as day and night from William Wilberforce, a highborn, polished individual who supped with kings and prime ministers. Newton, from the lower slum districts, was a slave trader.

Wilberforce had heard that Newton was a brave man with an indomitable spirit who used to captain a ship that brought slaves from Africa to the Western world. Then one day, God dramatically got hold of his life, and Newton became a minister, known for his great hymns of faith, such as "Amazing Grace."

Wilberforce was sure Newton would advise him to resign his position and study the Bible. He was "taken aback when Newton said he must serve Christ in his God-given post, if England was to ever become a Christian nation."

Into the equation of his life came another great friend and classmate, William Pitt. In his mid-twenties, Pitt was prime minister of England. The two became close, but Pitt was not a believer. Gifted as a parliamentarian, he had another cause in his heart. One he wanted to transfer to Wilberforce. The cause was slave trading.

This was not the first time Wilberforce was confronted with this problem. When he was still in his teens he had written an article for a newspaper urging the English to disengage from the abominable trade. It had no effect. John Newton had brought the tragedy to him, and now William Pitt had challenged him to do something about it. Wilberforce felt that God was impressing him with a cause.

He recognized his popularity would be doomed if he took the issue of slavery to Parliament. It was a source of great economic gain, and he knew many of his fellow politicians were involved. Spending hours in prayer, he felt obligated to God to form organizations that would address slavery and a moral realignment of England. Neither would be popular issues.

In 1787 he formed two societies, one for the abolition of the slave trade and the other for the reformation of manners. Some call it the first introduction of a moral majority. Wilberforce was known to the upper-class tailors in London. He had specific orders for his suits, instructing his tailor to add several additional pockets to his coats and fit some extra ones in his suits. He carried a library on his person.

After his death, it was discovered he had charts plotting every day. In small segments he would indicate the time he spent in prayer, study, what was needed for Parliament, and how to better address the slave issue. Faithfulness was his first priority. Doing what Jesus Christ would do in every circumstance of life was his hourly challenge. He was a proponent of truth and modeled righteousness. Historians say Wilberforce could have been prime minister, but he put that position aside with the message that "when called to do the work of the Lord, never stoop to being a prime minister."

Years passed and his dedication grew. When he first went to Parliament he knew of no other Christian who was given over to God. When he found the Lord, he worked diligently. When he left office, there were more than one hundred Christians in each of the houses of Parliament. His writings were read by the upper class he knew well, and one of his books with a twenty-five-word, noncatchy title went into twenty-one editions and is available today.

Being formed in the image of Christ was not easy for Wilberforce. He was maligned and ridiculed, but he outlived it all because of the outworking of Christ in his life. He was determined and devoted to prepare to be the bride of Christ.

His faithfulness set a standard for others. His very life, without words, asked others to follow him as he followed Christ. He fought slavery for almost six decades. He suffered a terminal illness just a short walk from the House of Commons where, before his death, at long last, the vote to end slavery was cast. The seven hundred thousand slaves of Britain were set free. His labor was not in vain. It was a feat accomplished decades before the slaves were freed by America's Emancipation Proclamation.

Wilberforce had his victories, but most of them were preceded by defeats. His oratorical, wrenching speeches, often lasting for hours, touched the parliamentarians but they still continued to defeat his pleas. He fought ill health his whole life. His stature was small, barely five feet tall; his head appearing heavy for his body as it often rested on his chest. But the one called a midget by his detractors was a towering giant in the kingdom of God. Even to the present day England has not had a racial uprising, although there are still class distinctions.

One of the lessons we need to learn from the life of a far-seeing man such as Wilberforce is not to run before the Lord in deciding what we will do with our lives. We need not be swayed by the opinions of others in making our choices. It is not necessary for everyone to go into the ministry to serve the Lord. Sometimes, it is enough that we remain in place, in service on His staff, and outserve, outwork, and outmodel others in His saving grace.

Jesus too was ridiculed, and people rejected His plea to come to Him and be set free from the slavery of sin. Some accept but all too lightly embrace their spiritual emancipation. Jesus is asking more. Come you blessed of My Father and inherit eternal life. We are born with a divine destiny. Finding yours and becoming faithful, preparing to become the bride of Christ.

Can Jesus count on you?

7

Get into the Prayer Closet

Even them will I bring to my holy mountain, and make them joyful in my house of prayer: their burnt offerings and their sacrifices shall be accepted upon mine altar; for mine house shall be called an house of prayer for all people.

Isaiah 56:7, KJV

oll Americans on the subject of God and you will discover that, by an overwhelming margin, they are very comfortable with and committed to a belief in God. This seems to be the state of the church as well. We are committed to our belief *of* God, but how deep is our belief *in* God? There is no shortage of people in the church who claim devotion to God, yet where can we look to see that devotion in action? If there truly are seventy million Evangelicals in America, as one poll suggested, then we have to ask ourselves, "What's wrong with us?" We can console ourselves by listing all the great ministries available, but let's take a candid look. This country is on a quick trip to hell if we don't have a visitation of God's Spirit that leads to spiritual awakening.

God moves by moving in the hearts of people. We serve the Lord of the breakthrough in the neglected area of personal devotion. God is calling us into the closet of intimacy with Him. In this set-apart time, God breaks through to our hearts. From this distinct and mandatory place of growth in Him, we not only experience our breakthrough, but we become available to seed breakthrough in other people's hearts. We become the fruit of the intentions of the Lord. As we surrender to Him, we become the offering that God gives on earth to a dying world. Do you claim devotion to God and rarely darken the door of your prayer closet? God is calling you to greater intimacy. He wants to take you to the deep waters of fellowship with Himself. Are you willing to answer the call of God to a new level of devotion?

We are salt and light. Our devotion leads us to becoming the "sought out" of Isaiah 62. "You shall be called Sought Out, A City Not Forsaken" (Isa. 62:12). The church becomes the New Jerusalem covering, resembling the bride, preparing to marry the Lord. It takes intense personal devotion toward the Lord to be sought out.

Who can measure the value of being called a man of God, or a woman of God? This was the declaration of God to both Abraham and Sarah, father and mother of nations. It happened through their obedience and personal devotion to God. They were broken through by the Lord and became the seed to bring many to Him, even into the present day.

No matter what circumstances drive the raging tempest in your life, the safest place to be is near to the heart of God. This is why, even in the midst of a great storm, Jesus could rest in the bottom of a boat. Being in His will is peace. Where do you learn of His heart and discern His will and destiny for your life? During quiet moments in your prayer closet seeking His face.

One of the great tragedies in the church is the shrinking heart syndrome. We become so much a part of the world we live in, so busy adding activity on top of activity, that we don't see what is really happening to our spiritual capacity. While we think that we are filling our lives with good things, we are actually stuffing our lives to the point that our hearts have to shrink to make room for our ever-increasing selves. Of all persons, Christians should have the largest hearts, the warmest embrace, and the most time for others.

Jesus said, "Give me your heart, I want to take it, make that stony heart pliable to be molded into My service for My kingdom." David prayed for an "enlarged heart." Jabez prayed for an "enlarged coast," with a heart to reach his generation. Great revivals are seeded from hearts totally broken for the work of God and yielded to the will of God.

Every Christian heart is the ground that God planned for service before the foundation of the world. He was forming you so that everything within you would fit everything that God had ordained in heaven. I want to remind you again that you are the New Jerusalem that came down from God out of heaven. The question is, Are you preparing your heart for service in the quietness of your devotional life?

For many Christians it would be an embarrassing moment if God called us to heaven for spiritual evaluation. How qualified for spiritual service in God's eyes would we be if everything about us was stripped away except our spiritual nature? What would be left to show God if our earthly nature was eliminated? No wealth, no possessions, no position—just our spiritual nature? What tools would we have? What spiritual treasures are stored to be utilized in His service? What have we consecrated for use to reign with Him? Would we be sadly deficient or equipped and ready because of our earthly preparation? Would we act like babies who have grown in body but display spiritually retarded growth?

God Doesn't Call the Qualified—He Qualifies the Called

In moments of spiritual appraisal sometimes we don't like what we see and hide behind the fig leaf of "I'm not qualified for that service to God." But God doesn't call the qualified. He qualifies the called. And you, Christian man and woman, *are* called.

I pray to God that my life will reflect the glory of His Son and the indescribable beauty of His bride. As an individual, a minister, and a writer, my intense desire is written in Psalm 45:1 (NASB): "My heart overflows with a good theme; I address my verses to the King; my tongue is the pen of a ready writer." I want my life to be like a best-selling book. When people who know me and hear me and discover truth that God has revealed to me, I hope they are driven to His heavenly bookstore and go to the shelf where Wellington Boone is displayed and want to read more about Christ. Not for personal honor, but because I displayed such a Godlike spirit the "book buyers" wanted to learn more about my Jesus and become better equipped to walk with and imitate Christ. When people open the book of your life, what do they read? Are the pages filled with information about you or do they cause readers to see Christ and crave to know more of the story?

Christian, you are telling a story about Jesus Christ. What a tragedy it would be if the narrative of your life led the reader away from the main plot. The book of our life in Christ is to be known and read of men, but if we continue walking after the flesh, instead of the Lord, we will be permanently shelved.

People often ask, How do I deepen my roots in God? There is something of which we can be sure. If you truly hunger and thirst for righteousness, *you will be filled*. The Bible declares it! There is an element of mystery to a deep consecration to God, but take James's advice. In the quietness of your prayer closet "Draw near to God and He will draw near to you" (James 4:8, NASB). Rely on the Holy Spirit to guide you into the deep channel of intimacy. We need to get quiet before God—a difficult thing in this society. Perhaps God is calling you to the wilderness. Go. Rid yourself of distractions. Focus on God. Read His Word. Listen to His Spirit. Praise His holy name. Magnify and honor Him as your sovereign Lord. Then, be still before His majesty.

We Are in Training for Eternity Right Now

We are in training for eternity now. Do not live below what God has foreordained for you. Heaven is a place prepared for us. At present, each heart is becoming a mansion. Inside there is beauty. Inside there is meekness. Hate does not fit. Selfishness does not have a corner in this residence. Spite, jealousy, and strife are not found in heaven because God says each body is a temple of the Holy Ghost. This has nothing to do with circumstances. Often circumstances do not change, but your heart can change. We can change our mind-sets and let the mind of Christ be in us.

The circumstances of my growing up are described in chapter 12. My résumé was fit for the ghetto, but God became the great ghetto buster. He is in the transforming business, not just for this little time we are on earth, but for heaven. You may not be listed in the Fortune 500, but you carry the name of Jesus, the creator of wealth and the sustainer of the universe. Such knowledge we must continue to feed into our spirits because we are becoming what we already are in Christ—perfect!

Even though we stand before God clean in Christ, He is continuing the process of perfecting our character here on earth. Through the ministry of suffering and times of deprivation, we are prepared for usefulness. We must meet these times aggressively and on our knees in our prayer closet.

We were saved, not just to avoid hell or to go to heaven, but to be conformed to the image of His Son during our stay upon the earth. His divine agenda is to make us like Himself, to be conformed and transformed. It happens through dying to self and suffering and pain.

> For it became him, for whom are all things, . . . in bringing many sons unto glory, to make the captain of their salvation perfect through sufferings. . . . For in that he himself hath suffered being tempted, he is able to succor them that are tempted.
>
> *Hebrews* 2:10, 18, KJV

Robert Foster, in *The Challenge*, paints a wonderful scenario of Peter. Impulsive Peter who knew suffering, but also the resultant joy through suffering. He wrote:

> When Peter saw the high waves he was terrified and began to sink. 'Save me, Lord!' he shouted. (Matthew 14:23–33)

Have you ever heard of Jean-Francois Gravelet? Perhaps you know of him by his pseudonym, Blondin, tightrope walker and acrobat from London, England.

Blondin crossed Niagara Falls a number of times on a wire, 1,100 feet long and 160 feet above the raging waters. He always did it with different theatrical variations: blindfolded, in a sack, pushing a wheelbarrow, on stilts, or carrying a man on his back.

Can you believe this one? Blondin got to the midway point above the Falls, sat down on a chair, cooked an omelette and ate it in a totally relaxed fashion. I want to remind you of Simon Peter who also did many praiseworthy things during the course of his lifetime, but this episode of walking upon the water must rank as one of his greatest.

No wire . . . no abracadabra . . . no yoga . . . no hidden rocks underneath. "Surrounded by obvious dangers, faced with utter impossibilities, Peter found inner strength in his Lord's command: 'Come.'" Peter, a sharer with his Master in the suspension of natural laws.

Then the whole project blew up at four o'clock in the morning. With his eyes on Jesus, Peter was walking on top of the storm; the next moment he was "in over his head." Soaked to the skin, Peter was rescued by Jesus. As had been well said, a saint is not a man who never falls; a saint is a man who gets up and goes on again every time he falls. Down but not out.

"Lord, save me!" No superfluous words, no unnecessary theology, no time to elaborate on details of why, no time to observe any ceremonial laws. "It is the quickest, easiest, and most desperate way to reach the heart of God." Sinking time is praying time. Failure is looking at self; Faith is riveted solely on Jesus.

Peter was not blamed:
for daring but for doubting.
not for failure, but for faltering.
not for lack of courage, but for lack of confidence.

You may not be a Blondin or Peter, but you are out there in the midst of the night and the storm is "contrary." Don't measure the waves, don't gauge the wind, don't give in to the danger, and, most of all, don't throw in the towel and sink under the circumstances. "Keep your eyes on Jesus, our leader and instructor . . . if you want to keep from becoming fainthearted and weary" (Heb. 12:3, TLB).

Toward the end of 1 Peter, the apostle wrote:

And after you have suffered for a little while, the God of all grace, who called you to His eternal glory in Christ, will

Himself perfect, confirm, strengthen and establish you. To Him be dominion forever and ever.

1 *Peter* 5:1, NASB

Peter knew brokenness. His was a rough and turbulent experience on the road of life as he sought to walk with God. In his triumphs and tribulations he was being perfected. Like an unfinished canvas of the master artist, God was remaking him. He said to him, "Peter, thou art, but thou shalt be." Peter was an example of the past (thou art) being formed into the future (thou shalt be). Again, God sees us not as we are but as He ordained us to be.

Jeremiah described the work of the master potter in our lives.

The word which came to Jeremiah from the LORD saying: "Arise and go down to the potter's house, and there I will cause you to hear my words." Then I went down to the potter's house, and there he was, making something at the wheel. And the vessel that he made of clay was marred in the hand of the potter; so he made it again into another vessel, as it seemed good to the potter to make. Then the word of the LORD came to me, saying: "O house of Israel, can I not do with you as this potter?" says the LORD. "Look, as the clay is in the potter's hand, so are you in My hand, O house of Israel."

Jeremiah 18:1–6

After his suffering, Peter learned that this God of all grace would "establish, strengthen, and settle him." He was literally established by being transformed and firmed up for service. Even his name was changed from Simon to Peter—translated as "rock." God "marred" Peter for His good pleasure. He was "strengthened" by putting on the armor of God and developing his spiritual muscles to keep on in the faith, even to the point of death.

Peter the rock had been shaken. He made the impulsive decision to meet Jesus on the water, argued all the way to the Last Supper, denied Jesus but was quick to admit his sinfulness. He rode out the storms with the God of all grace. Grace is not free. God gave His life for it. Its availability equipped Peter, even after his sin, and it equips us only as we are in the face of Jesus. Have you closed the closet door to get alone with God?

If we are to build the city of God, it must be built to divine specifications. Part of the qualification of every laborer is suffering for His sake. With suffering is the accompanying promise that those who suffer with Him shall reign with Him. We can reign with Him only if we suffer with Him. Why? Because it is through submission to Christ in suffering that we come to rely on Him, and God will only give governance to those who rely on Him. Isaiah illustrated this: "In returning and rest you shall be saved; in quietness and in confidence shall be your strength" (Isa. 30:15).

The context of this truth appears when the Israelites were faced with trouble. They made a decision to pledge their allegiance with the nations that surrounded them, including Egypt. They had forgotten their source of strength was in the Lord, and only in returning to Him would they be saved.

Not long ago, in Tyler, Texas, a tragic automobile accident left a beautiful sixteen-year-old girl as a quadriplegic. She was faced with a difficult choice at an early age. She could let this circumstance ruin her or use it to reign with Christ. She chose to look to God's Word: "He knoweth the way that I take; when he hath tried me, I shall come forth as gold" (Job 23:10, KJV). For thirty-five years she has been confined to a wheelchair, but the chair does not define her. The suffering and loss of mobility are not her focus. She learned, even with diminished strength, that she could reach out to children and adults and minister Christ's love to them on the telephone. With a specially made device, she is able to hold the receiver and share the good gospel news. Clowns at area circuses carry her phone number to give to latchkey children. Many people call with the names of kids who need help. She spends untold hours on the phone talking about Jesus.

She has been hammered and forged, passed into the heat of affliction and pain again and again, but the product is finished, polished, and ready for each delicate task God gives her. The God of all grace, after she has suffered, is making her perfect through suffering, and she is giving others an example to follow. Her success has come through brokenness, which she turned around for the glory of God. She chose to draw near to God in her physical tragedy.

Like Job, she did not say, "I know the way God takes," instead she affirms, "He knows the way that I take." It would be wonderful to better understand what God sees if we could pull away the veil and glimpse the end as well as the interim.

Every Place of Desperation Is the Door to Restoration

Even though many Christians let suffering destroy their faith, this is not its purpose. As we take our suffering into the prayer closet with God we learn to allow our faith to be strengthened. God takes us to places where He allows us to be desperate. Get into the closet. In hearing our cry, He knows if we are in earnest and then He reveals Himself. God creates desperation in your heart for a purpose. Every place of desperation is the door to restoration. The Bible calls it hunger and thirst.

I have learned that if I am to break through to deeper intimacy with God, I cannot seek manifestation, but I must seek tenderness of heart so God can move upon me to become more yielded. That is what God is looking for, a yielded life. Once you surrender, you will find He is there for you. The sacrifice of a broken and contrite heart He does not overlook. Such revelation relates to death. Revelation always requires a new dependency and a new sacrifice, because the will of God is usually the opposite of your personal desire.

Consider the second chapter of Mark where there is a narrative about four men who brought a paralyzed man to Jesus. They gained entrance by breaking through a roof above a sold-out crowd who came to hear Jesus. It took courage to break in, but their confidence level was so high, they knew Jesus would meet them. They were hungry and thirsty, and their friend was healed.

When the apostle Paul was a prisoner, he was en route by ship to Rome to appear before Caesar. The ship was caught in a storm and destroyed. We have an insight into a faithful God through reading the story. Obviously, many of the passengers could swim, but for those without life preservers, the Word notes, "And the rest, some on boards, and some on broken pieces of the ship. And so it came to pass, that they escaped all safe to land" (Acts 27:44, KJV).

When the ship broke up and the waves washed over the heads of those in the water, there were pieces of the ship, boards, and hatch covers to which they could cling, keeping them buoyant until they reached shore. Even in the most turbulent times God will always provide something for us to hold on to. He is like that. He promises pieces of safety in our storms, literally an ark of safety through His Son.

Another broken object in the Bible is the broken vase. Mark 14 relates a beautiful story of a woman who broke an alabaster box of perfume to pour on Jesus' feet. Here was a profile of a woman who wanted to show her love and devotion overtly. The story pictures a woman who put herself and her possession on the altar for Jesus. Often we lay our lives on the altar and then get right back up. God is looking for the kind of witnesses who lay it all out for God, like the martyrs of old whose death brought new life to the church. Witness means martyr.

Today when you look at the universal body of Christ, there appears to be such a small remnant who are seriously committed to God. Few have His intensity. It has often been asked, Who knows the impact of one life totally surrendered to God? When I speak to a great crowd, I look out on a sea of faces and pray that God will touch even one. If one person hears the Lord, that could make a difference to a whole generation. One person, wholly sold out to Him, ready and willing to pour out all, like the devotion represented by the alabaster box on the feet of Jesus. God is calling you into the closet of devotion to Him. Won't you identify yourself with the remnant of those wholly devoted to Christ, ready, prepared, and willing to do the will of the Father?

If We Choose to Be Stiffnecked, God May Give Us What We Want

Remember when the people of Israel told Samuel that they wanted a king just like the kingdoms around them? Samuel knew this would anger God. He did not want to miss God's voice. The people were not satisfied with what God was doing. After he warned the people of what an earthly king would really mean, they were unrelenting. So God gave them their desire, which ultimately turned into disaster.

Probably one of the most dreadful things God can do for us is give us the desires of our flesh. But if we complain enough,

He will do it, as history (and very likely your own experience) has demonstrated. God let the Israelites harvest the fruit of their self-centered lives. He'll let you do it, too. After a while, He took things back into His own plan and handpicked David.

In David, God saw things that related to the character of Jesus because He is called David's greatest son. All through David's life we see the God of the breaking through. David, having been God's choice, was a spiritual choice. He was a spiritual man who was going to represent a certain character or quality in Jesus that we are to embrace today. Qualities of devotion, developed in times of breaking and suffering.

One of those qualities appears in 1 Chronicles 12:1 (KJV): "Now these are they that came to David to Ziklag . . . because of Saul." This is significant for us to see because Saul represents the flesh. David restricted himself because of the flesh. Exactly the same reason we do. The way to overcome the flesh is by restricting it, by restricting your own motivations that are fleshly. David waited until these men came to him at Ziklag. He was proven to be a mighty man of battle and had occasion to be able to defeat Saul numerous times because it was God who had anointed him king. David was modeling his humbleness, that he would not do anything to exalt himself. David restricted himself.

Christians need a new understanding of those qualities of life that David possessed, enabling him to be king. We must understand in these latter days that all exaltation comes from God. He is not giving you an opportunity for self-aggrandizement or self-esteem in giving you position in Him. He wants only to provide you with self-worth by giving you an inner change. David illustrates this by being on the back side of the mountain, tending sheep. He was the least expected to be exalted, the youngest of the brothers. He already knew what it was to be lowly.

He had reason to gloat about all the leaders coming to him about his defeat of Saul, anointing him as king, but he restricted himself. The example goes further with Jesus. When they sought to make Him king, what did He do? He restricted Himself because He came to minister as a prophet and to be a propitiation for the world. He came to earth to go down, to die, and in His going down and dying He was exalted and made King of kings and Lord of lords.

We are required to hold that principle as a lifestyle. God is the promoter, and the way we are promoted in the kingdom of God is by learning to restrict the self-life.

Man desires to be valued but is unsure what constitutes real value. If you study values clarification, you will learn that man is not clear as to what he values because the foundational base is disrupted. The foundation was destroyed because God, the creator of life, is the only one who defines value. Without knowing the source of value, they can only be shaped by personal criteria.

We see this further broken down in picturing the mighty men of David who were qualified and proven in battle, thus gaining recognition in their past accomplishment. They were awesome in terms of their physical prowess and battlefield résumés. What would it be like for the top military echelon to be put on alert and sent to be on your side? They were chosen, the best out of every tribe of Israel. With them David could rely on natural ability. Could you restrict yourself as David did?

Jesus said, "You don't take my life, I lay my life down." Jesus could have called out the whole host of heaven, but by a volitional act He was willing to die.

Notice David doing the same. He had every ability to capture the kingdom with the reserves waiting to fight for him, those mighty men of war. David knew this was a war in a different dimension. It was a war between the flesh and the spirit.

God ordained that David would be king. He had sent His prophet to anoint him from among his brethren. With such knowledge wouldn't it have been logical to use the men God had provided to claim the throne? Why was it necessary for him to restrict himself when it was God's will for him to be king? Why did he choose not to use his forces? Because he walked in the knowledge he developed through brokenness and maintained his priorities. It was David who proclaimed in Psalm 75:6–7: "For exaltation comes neither from the east nor from the west nor from the south. But God is the Judge: He puts down one and exalts another!"

David surrendered to the purposes of God. He didn't seek his own personal victory. He was committed to God and knew the key to his being king was based not on his abilities, but his availability. In God's kingdom, the greatest ability is availability. David modeled for us that his being king was God's accomplishing His purpose through divine strength. He accepted the reality that as long as Saul still had the throne, it was not time. David concerned himself with God's time clock, not his own.

Consider David as he moved into God's plan for him when he was broken. He related, "The cords of death encompassed me, and the terrors of Sheol came upon me; I found distress and sorrow" (Ps. 116:3–4, NASB). In Psalm 42 we learn he was broken and his soul was cast down. He was in exile and yearned to return to Jerusalem. In the depths of his distress, he knew where to turn. He remembered the Lord and found the grace of God that took him through and over the trial.

Deep calls to deep at the sound of Thy waterfalls; All Thy breakers and Thy waves have rolled over me. The LORD will command His lovingkindness in the daytime; and His song will be with me in the night.

Psalm 42:7–8, NASB

Here was a man with a song in the night, having experienced distress in the daylight. Why? He had a right relationship to his trial because of God. His cast-down countenance found hope in God, and as he praised God, his countenance got the message.

Submission to brokenness develops character within us. In our personal devotion, God reveals the very nature of our hearts. The worst thing that could happen would be if God did not reveal our sinful nature. When you close the door of your prayer closet, pray Psalm 51 before God with humble contrition.

> Behold, I was brought forth in iniquity, and in sin my mother conceived me. Behold, Thou dost desire truth in the innermost being, and in the hidden part Thou wilt make me know wisdom.
>
> Psalm 51:5–6, NASB

The spirit is the discerner of our very thoughts and just how serious we are in breaking through to God and in allowing Him to break through to us. As we yield, He comes to forgive, refresh, and send you out as His champion.

Prayer is the channel of change. Until we are dedicated to God, He says there is no value in His giving His visions and dreams to us. I often ask audiences, "What would your city be like if everyone was just the same as you, still harboring the things that break God's heart? Today He is giving you a chance to change, to grow up in Him through purity and devotion."

We Can't Go to Church—We Are the Church

We have a distorted view of what this Christian life is all about. Just being religious, just going to church will land you in hell. True believers cannot just go to church, they are the church!

Don't attempt to fulfill mere religious duty. Devote yourself to the cause of Christ until the reality of the Lord is working inside you. We are in a kingdom, a real world. Unless the Lord opens our eyes, there is no way we can see. Jesus said the kingdom of God is near. This is not a geographic location. It is a place you come to in your vision of God and He opens your eyes through His Word, as the word becomes, not just print on pages, but the living, vital words of life.

In many services I have asked for the perfect people in the congregation to stand up. I am still waiting for the first response. We all know the truth only too well. We are still committing sins of omission and commission. We reject doing what we know is right and directly sin by doing what is wrong. We hear the word and it does not take root. We may be born again, but we are not serious. We have a tendency to repent again and again of the same things that keeps God from reinvading our lives. But our hope never fails. Our destiny in God is wrapped up in obedience. "If you love Me, you will keep My commandments" (John 14:15, NASB).

It's Crunch Time in the Church

It's crunch time in the church. It takes time, thought, contrition, and devotion to develop into the image of God. It takes prayer and supplication to be changed. I urge you to take the ball now. Don't pass it to someone else. God's heart is anxious to invest substance in your life and to bring you to maturity. The church has been languishing at babyhood level for too long. This generation can only be changed through a renewed level of seriousness modeled in devotion to Christ.

What does your name speak to this generation? Can God put your name on the list with Abraham, Isaac, and Jacob. What does it represent to heaven? Could you build a generation and

nething from nothing. I was in His mind before I under-
od who I was. The outworking of His mind through me
hs ministries because this is not a religion or a man, it is
word from God.

passionately encourage you to let the Lord break through
our life and then discover within your heart the ability to
ite something from nothing. God wants you to see what is
sible in the body of Christ. As it comes into manifestation,
not change your mind. Hold fast to the insight God gives
. Let your life be an awesome expression of the will of the
d so when people see you they will know, beyond doubt,
e is a living God. God challenges. Lift up your eyes and
 from the place where you are. He did not say look where
are. Many of the problems with us today are that we look
re we are, rather than looking *from* where we are. We cannot
s on a problem and the answer at the same time. The Lord
 the end from the beginning. He invites us to extend our
n, reaching far into the horizon of God.

y consistent prayer is that Father God will cause my heart
e broken and receptive, ready for revelation, and ready to
g into maturity the words spoken into the womb of my
t. If there is even a pinpoint of His light within you, it is
igh to begin. The smallest glimmer of light dispels the
ness. Our world is overburdened with people who are
ed in darkness, seeking light. Isaiah described this when
rote, "The people who walked in darkness have seen a
t light; those who dwelt in the land of the shadow of
h, upon them a light has shined" (Isa. 9:2). Have you pene-
d that darkness and broken through with the light of His
and forgiveness?

rough our brokenness and devotion, the Lord deals with
challenge you to go on with Him. Many say I am too strict.
tell me I present a path and a God too hard for them to

cause their lives to be devout and committed
basis of your personal devotion? How familiar
heaven?

I challenge you to be in the face of God and
serious in your commitment to Christ. Do not
pastor pray for more people than you do. Do no
used for God more than you are useful to Him.
is called to have influence. There are people
God within you. Out of the loins of your spirit
leaders. It is true!

God told Abraham and Sarah that nations wo
their union. We become devoted and broker
raised up to be spiritual mothers and fat
Abraham and Sarah.

I think of Jackie Pullinger, a Mother Teresa–t
the vision of God to go into the walled cities ir
was totally at risk. Through her devoutness
spirit, thousands are being changed. She went
knowing where she was going. She launched c
in a boat without oars, trusting the winds of th
her. Knowing nothing of the culture or langua
she was among, she nevertheless walked in th
of God. Before she could even verbally share Je
changed by her modeling Him. Having learne
she moved into greater realms of humility a
God, without fear for her life, which is constan

This is what the kingdom is all about. Man
no comprehension of what I am sharing. The
of any destiny for their lives. They live wit
tomorrow or another life. But God is calling
better, something deeper.

This is my rule of faith and the way I order
my life when I realized He is in the bus

follow. I must respond to that. God never promised an easy road, but a higher road. There is no such thing as partial obedience. Partial obedience is disobedience.

I thank God that my serious conviction is being accepted by more in this time than in the past. His truths are taking root in good soil. This is the hour for true Christians to step forward. We are all together in this pilgrimage of going into the city and preparing for the city of God. My city! God does not need silver and gold to build the city. He has all that. His currency is people. He has created people who are to be made in the likeness of His Son. His people. He rejoices over them and shares the riches of eternity with them. But He does not give out adult things to children. As long as you remain a child, you are unqualified for the heritage that is offered to you.

Get into the closet and ask God for more of Himself and more of His Spirit, more of His power and glory and more of His anointing. It is found in the upper room of commitment, where the disciples were told to wait until they were endued with power from on high.

One of the places where David experienced the victory of God was named Baal-Perazim, which means, "The Lord of the breakings through." Daily we are given the challenge of being broken and tested, to be quickened with new mercy and fresh, unexpected surprises. Through our faithful commitment, restriction of self, and devotion, a faithful God reveals Himself specifically to our individual need. We point to a place called Baal-Perazim, where our faithful Father broke through!

8

Blessed Beyond Measure

Now unto him that is able to do exceeding abundantly above all that we ask or think, according to the power that worketh in us, unto him be glory in the church by Christ Jesus throughout all ages, world without end.

Ephesians 3:20–21, KJV

There is a great hunger in today's society for truth and reality. You have read that I often say to an audience, "Are you hungry?" The response is overwhelming! There is a famine in the lives of many Christians that can be stopped. I call it a Word famine. God has given us His Word to feast upon. It alone satisfies the hungering soul. I understand because this hunger and thirst for more of God and a growing desire to bring people to His table of abundance remains inside me.

Food in the Bible pertains to what we eat spiritually. We eventually become what we eat. If we are healthy, we most likely choose to eat healthy food. An unhealthy diet leads to poor health. The same reality is true biblically as well. Where I am spiritually is based on the kind of food I eat and digest.

One day the disciples came to Jesus concerned about His mealtime. They sought Him out and said, "Master, eat." He answered, "I have meat to eat that ye know not of." The disciples said one to another, "Hath any man brought him aught to eat?" Jesus said, "My meat is to do the will of him that sent me, and to finish his work" (John 4:31–34, KJV). What is so powerful about the Lord's response is that Jesus was giving them a reason for eating. It was clear He had no motivation for physical food if it was not to strengthen Him to be able to do the will of His Father.

Without a sense of destiny, He said, there was no reason to live. Being fully aware of His destiny, cause, and purpose, the physical food eaten to sustain Him better enabled Him to work the works of His Father in heaven. It was previously revealed that He had eaten from the intentions of the Lord. He was committed to His purpose in coming to earth, which was the real food provided by heaven. If He was not accomplishing His divine destiny and modeling the principles of God and the ways of God, He had no motivation to eat physical food.

Jesus mentioned not just food, but meat. In 1 Corinthians 3, the Bible talks about the different levels of food—milk, sincere milk, meat, and strong meat. Hebrews is often described as a book for spiritually mature Christians.

> Of whom we have much to say, and hard to explain, since you have become dull of hearing. For though by this time you ought to be teachers, you need someone to teach you again the first principles of the oracles of God; and you have come to need milk and not solid food.
>
> *Hebrews* 5:11–12

This is significant because we have talked about serving the Lord for His hands, meaning we often possess a consumer's mentality. We look for a handout, for God to give us something more tangible than Himself. Jesus said we ought to be teachers. He wants us to serve as His feet so we will take our proper place, not as a consumer, but as abundant suppliers. Maturity is a place where we are challenged to give out the food of life that digests into reason and purpose and can be used to feed others.

When you consider milk, sincere milk, meat, and strong meat, you are talking about what you are eating spiritually. So, on the one hand, when listening to the Word, what is being said should help lead you and give you direction. It must also equip you to be aware of what the Lord is saying, where His Word is taking you, and from it, what you are becoming in Him. The food of your understanding is provided to bring you to the place where you are no longer babies, but adults. A diet of milk represents spiritual regression. Strong meat belongs to those who are full of spiritual maturity. It is not an age issue. God will give His deep things to those who are ready to hear Him, no matter how young.

What we eat and how we exercise is the basis of our walk with the Lord. It is what keeps us focused and directed on all that the Lord said we should do in obedience. Become partakers of the right food and you will not waver. It is the right spiritual food that leads to breaking through in areas of destiny, family, personal devotion, reconciliation, and revival.

When we look at the cry for reconciliation, we look at the meaning of what Paul said: eat the food of unity, the fruit of unconditional love, compassion, and mercy. That divine nutrition will give you the strength and ability to follow through on God's intentions.

The Puritans used to sing:

> Oh, let me undistracted be,
> To watch and work and wait for Thee.

With anticipation of that day, they feasted on the Lord. I encourage you to feed on spiritual meat, enabling you to move on to become the one the Lord uses to bring others into their God-ordained destiny.

There are four things that I practice to stay in there with the Lord. First, I must desire to be relationally in there with Him. If

I am out of fellowship with God, there is a reason. Sin. I have to confess to God the sins that I commit. This is an imperative step to fellowship. Another way to be out of fellowship is to fail to stay in contact. Just like two people who were friends at one time but grew apart when one of them moved away and stopped writing and calling, so we can grow apart from God. We have to stay in touch with God through prayer on a regular basis. Think about your relationship to God right now. Are you in or out of fellowship with Him? If the answer is out, the road back is through repentance and prayer.

Another way I stay in there with the Lord is a desire to be quick to obey. The Hebrews taught intrinsic hearing—hearing that leads to obedience. In this country, our hearing is not always that way. Americans tend to believe they have heard when all they have done is listen to someone or read something on a particular subject. Hebrew thinking is being convinced you have not really heard until you adhere to what was presented. Obedience is built in. I believe hearing involves proving to God, by your actions, that you really have heard. It is what Jesus was teaching when He said, "If you love me you will keep my commandments." This works out in faith and obedience, which are synonymous.

The third activity I use to stay close to the Lord is to be quick to forgive. When you stand praying, if you have not forgiven your brother his trespasses, neither has your heavenly Father forgiven you of yours. It is crucial as you walk with the Lord to do so with a sense of confidence. The word is clear:

> If we confess our sins, He is faithful and just to forgive our sins, and to cleanse us from all unrighteousness.
>
> 1 John 1:9, NASB

Forgiveness is prerequisite to walking with a clear conscience. Unwillingness to forgive has been described as slow suicide.

The fourth practice that helps me walk closely with God is seeking a sense of holiness in maintaining a pure thought life. It is important that we recognize that we are not delivered from temptation, we just do not have to yield to the temptation that comes to us. Sometimes people get confused. Men and women may have problems with sexual thoughts. However, if these thoughts are brought under the blood, in and of themselves, they are not sin. It is when the thoughts are allowed to stay and germinate. The Bible teaches us to cast down imaginations.

People have said to me that I am a bad person because I think bad things. No, the devil can seed into us bad thoughts. The Bible says we are to give no place to the devil. Do not claim the thought as yours. Cast it out and put it out of your mind. Feed yourself with His Word. He tells us that:

Whatever things are true, whatever things are noble, whatever things are just, whatever things are pure, whatever things are lovely, whatever things are of good report . . . meditate on these things.

Philippians 4:8

Do not tell yourself these thoughts are yours. The devil percolates them through your mind. Purify your mind. Let your heart repudiate your mind's being a place where the devil could even consider attempting to feed into it God-dishonoring thoughts. Wash yourself with the water of the Word. Through the input of the Word, fill your mind with good things. Reaffirm in your thought processes what the Bible says in 2 Corinthians 5:21, "For He made Him who knew no sin to be sin for us, that we might become the righteousness of God in Him." Confirm who you are. Even say aloud, as I do, "I am the righteousness of God in Christ. I am pure as He is pure. I walk in virtue because He has given me a new nature. Christ is in me, and because He is in me, I am clean." Saying those things is helpful. It becomes speaking the word, and the Bible says, "By your words are you justified" (Matt. 12:37). "That the sharing of your faith may become effective [energized] by the acknowledgment of every good thing that is in you in Christ Jesus" (Philem. 1:6).

Continually reaffirm who you are in Christ and the contract you have made with Him to walk wholly pleasing to Him in all holiness.

Personal devotion has both an inward part and the practical part. Both are needed to strengthen our commitment during our quiet time with our God. The Old Testament presented commands to remember who the Lord was. This was later reaffirmed by Jesus Himself.

> Every commandment which I command you today you must be careful to observe, that you may live and multiply, and go in and possess the land which the LORD swore to your fathers. And you shall remember that the LORD your God led you all the way these forty years in the wilderness, to humble you and test you, to know what was in your heart, whether you would keep His commandments or not. So He humbled you, allowed you to hunger, and fed you with manna which you did not know nor did your fathers know, that He might make you know that man shall not live by bread alone; but man lives by every word that proceeds from the mouth of the LORD.
>
> *Deuteronomy* 8:1–3

Hearing, as taught from the Hebrew and Greek perspective, is hearing and living by, not the letter of the word—mere hearing, but listening and doing. The letter kills but the spirit gives life. Jesus said, "'Who do you say that I am?' Simon Peter answered and said, 'You are the Christ, the Son of the Living God.' Jesus answered and said to him, 'Flesh and blood has not revealed this to you, but My Father who is in heaven'" (Matt. 16:15–17). The defining word is "revealed." Hearing has to do with the revealed word. Man does not live by the legalistic letter, but by the revelation of the Word. As you go into the Word to read the Word, be aware, the Word is reading you. That corresponds with teaching that says, "the Word of God is as a glass." The Greek further clarifies the meaning by likening it to, "the mirror that tries our thoughts."

> For the word of God is living and powerful, and sharper than any two-edged sword, piercing even to the division of soul and spirit, and of joints and marrow, and is a discerner of the thoughts and intents of the heart.
>
> *Hebrews* 4:12

The Word of God cuts right to the innermost intimacy of your heart and allows you to see your very own nature through the face of Jesus Christ. This brings you the correction process, because without spiritual discernment how can you repent of something Jesus has not yet shown you?

As you are reading the revealed Word, the Lord comes to you and is showing you the status of your heart. He allows the mirror to reflect where you are out of line, and you are convicted as to where repentance is needed. In repenting, restoration is assured as described in Acts 3:19: "Repent therefore and be converted, that your sins may be blotted out, so that times of refreshing may come from the presence of the Lord."

Personal devotion further brings a sense of the Lord to you. Even as Brother Lawrence wrote in his notes while preparing *Practice of the Presence of God*, "Closing in on God brings a heightened awareness of His majesty and holiness, diffusing His light into our most intimate dwelling places, flooding our souls with His preeminence and omniscience."

From that hallowed place, you are prepared to walk with a renewed sense of who He is and move confidently with the Lord into your daily affairs.

I have shared with many individuals who have come out of a theological seminary. They often explain that, while being in the hothouse of studying about God, they have experienced a dryness in their prayer life and walk with the Lord. They are laden down with thoughts and philosophies and interpretations of others. They want to know how to "hear" from God. But you can't hear the voice of God through the Scriptures if your ears are already full of other noise.

We must learn from the example of the children of Israel. God would only respond to them when they were devoted and obedient to Him. The same is true of us when we open the Word of God to hear from Him. We must pray that the eyes of our understanding will be enlightened and ask the Holy Spirit for specific direction. Let your expectation be of Him who is able to do exceedingly abundantly above all we ask or think. That is what revelation is all about.

I recommend five practical steps in personal devotion: hearing the Word, reading it, studying it, memorizing it, and meditating upon it. These are areas with biblical foundation and principles.

However, the spiritual is not first, but the natural, and afterward the spiritual (1 Cor. 15:46). One may not be at the place where revelation or walking with the spirit is understood. What do you do? You start natural. Then the Lord takes you to the spiritual. Diligently read the Bible every day. Through-the-Bible-in-a-year programs are good in the beginning. Remember to ask God, like the Hebrews did, to help you discern. As you read, read prayerfully. Some say they do not read the Scriptures, they pray the Scriptures. Let the Word leap into your heart. Believe that the Word will become manna to you, rich food for the day.

Ask the Lord to speak to you so there is no doubt within you about what you are reading. Then you will notice it moves from reading a mental treatise to a sense of the Lord speaking to you personally.

Study involves studying to show ourselves approved to God. One translation says we are to "concentrate on winning His approval." Studying the Word is like going to college to prepare for life. When it comes to the Word, we really are studying for our final exams. It takes time and work. Often Christians spend a couple of hours a week in church and depend on the speaker or pastor to enlighten them with the Word as it has been given to him. Sunday teaching is good but limited; it is not your own study. The benefit of a complete Bible study is made clear in Jeremiah 31:34.

No more shall every man teach his neighbor, and every man his brother, saying, "Know the LORD," for they all shall know me, from the least of them to the greatest of them, says the LORD. For I will forgive their iniquity, and their sin I will remember no more.

That does not exclude the teachers. It encourages us all toward personal, diligent study. God's commandments are not recommendations. The reward for faithfulness is truth and insight, and those very commands to study carry with them glorious promises of God.

In our study we are blessed to have the Holy Spirit, the resident truth teacher, as our helper.

The anointing which you have received from Him abides in you, and you do not need that anyone teach you; but as the same anointing teaches you concerning all things, and is true, and is not a lie, and just as it has taught you, you will abide in Him.

1 John 2:27

What You Eat Is What You Live By

Memorization is vital. David instructed by saying, "Thy word have I hid in my heart, that I might not sin against thee" (Ps. 119:11, KJV). Committing Scripture to memory is important because then our lives can be guided by those points. I have found it helpful to never memorize at random. I waited until the Lord gave me revelation in my reading and study, giving me something that specifically applied to me. Then I memorized those Scriptures because they moved me beyond merely quoting the passages to actually eating the Scripture, storing them for future use. What you have eaten is what you will live by. What is exciting is what follows. You become the fruit of that food. Fruit that can be fed to others. The Scripture is then working for you because, when you have digested it, in your explanation of it, it becomes what is integral in you and what you live by. As kind begets kind, so life produces life.

Meditation, at times, is likened to a cow that chews its cud. Meditation and prayer are vital. An example is discovered in Ezekiel.

I will give you a new heart and put a new spirit within you; I will take the heart of stone out of your flesh, and give you a heart of flesh. I will put My Spirit within you and cause you to walk in My statutes, and you will keep My

Judgments and do them. . . . I will also let the house of Israel inquire of Me to do this for them.

Ezekiel 36:26–27, 37

The Koreans, once they hear the word of the Lord in a church service, usually will not go out to eat like we do on Sundays or after prayer meetings. They refrain from putting food into themselves because they are convinced their appetites could take them into a carnal realm. They spend quality time praying the Scriptures into themselves. After hearing the word, they meditate hours later on the pastor's truths. One dear Korean sister said that when the services are over, "I go to pray, contemplate, pray, contemplate, keep it up until the good word takes root in my starving-for-more-of-Jesus heart." Prayerful meditation is chewed and digested and then brought back up as an offering unto the Lord. Revelation is often multiplied by prayer.

A teenager in Chicago came home from a youth group, excited about the word of the Lord. He told his father he could not go with the family to the local McDonald's for lunch because he was suffering from indigestion. The father was concerned and confused. The youngster explained the leader in church had presented the five steps of getting a grip on God as a five-course meal. The only way the class could get a solid grip on God was to feed themselves every day with this regimen of growing strong in the Lord and in the power of His might.

To illustrate, the teacher put a Bible on his hand. He explained that one cannot hold or grasp the Bible with one finger. It could be balanced, but easily upset. The finger represented hearing the Word. He then placed a second finger underneath, explaining that hearing and reading gave a better grip. But there was more. As he added each of the five fingers, representing hearing, reading, studying, memorizing, and meditating, he grasped the Bible and asked if any person in his class could take it out of his hand. They couldn't. Even the strongest in the class could not pull the Bible from his grasp as long as it was gripped by all five fingers. A son sowed into his dad how vital it was to maintain a firm grip on the Word. The family could go for hamburgers; he wanted to eat what he had learned!

Only thirteen years old, that boy started teaching high school released-time Christian education classes. He was hungry and discovered a secure foundation for his life. He modeled living evidence that blessed beyond measure is the young man whose delight is in the law of the Lord, one who meditates day and night in that law and brings forth its fruit (cf. Ps. 1:1–3).

If you are God's child He desires to bless you beyond measure. God is sending out a call to America. Will you choose to be one of the few who answer His call and devote your heart to Him? Choose today to take the hand of God and let His Spirit lead you to the high road of spiritual depth, the place where God prepares the hearts of those who will fulfill His purpose and receive His blessing.

A Blessed Beyond Measure devotion guide is outlined in appendix 3.

9

Sharpened Awareness

Behold, I will make thee a new sharp threshing instrument having teeth: thou shalt thresh the mountains, and beat them small, and shalt make the hills as chaff. . . . That they may see, and know, and consider, and understand together, that the hand of the Lord hath done this, and the Holy One of Israel hath created it.

Isaiah 41:15, 20, KJV

A good many years ago a man came into the church in Richmond, Virginia. We had discussed what it meant to come short of the glory of God—glory being defined as truly honoring God. He remembered the message I had given on men missing in action. He had taken it to heart and began developing a life that would not fall short of honoring God.

The next time we were brought together was at a church in Detroit. The words in his letter were potent and distinct:

I am no longer AWOL from the work of heaven. Long gone is my form of godliness. I have tapped into the circuitry of God. The world refuses to give me credence, but I am not daunted. My formerly cherished independence has been long lost into dependence on Father God and my family is seeking to please God through our lifestyle, doing as best we can to model Jesus.

I wanted to tell you, Wellington Boone, the first time I heard you I felt you were legalistic and harsh. In time, I realized, so was Jesus. He cast the moneychangers out of the temple. You cast my wishy-washy ways as a Christian out of my life as you led me into His book. First to prove you wrong, then to affirm that you are right. Keep it up. It works! God works! I am hoping to get a jurisdiction somewhere in your vicinity in the kingdom! Let's never become lax or fall short in honoring God.

The letter brought back memories of those sermons. I am convinced the church today comes up short in honoring God. There is a form of God there, but His real power is denied. Christianity tends to project a sense of independence, as this man had experienced. There is an outward display of honoring God, but not so strong that it causes the world to give credence to or honor what the Bible teaches. In fact, the world makes a conscious choice to relegate us to left field.

The world tends to be leery when committed Christians are involved in government or business. They feel more comfortable when church affairs are kept inside the church walls. They want economics, social reform, commerce, and education to remain untouched by the church. They want abject liberty and total security at the same time.

The high-stakes game they are in is seen in the life of a newborn. At birth when independence is finally achieved, the baby begins to cry for protection and security. Complete liberty leads to the desert and complete security is stifling. So, as life goes on, most people wander in perpetual conflict between the two without defining their conflict, and so it never becomes resolved. Decisions become constant balancing acts between being safe and being free.

The church has made a fine art of developing this secular conflict of wanting to be independent and free while still wanting to be secure in the faith. Many Christians are so worried about maintaining their freedom in Christ that they forget about the chains of the gospel. Independent from what? The claims of Christ on your life? We are saved, but we fall short of honoring God by not possessing the mind of Christ. It turns out that even though we are saved and are good people, there are many in the world who do not subscribe to Christ, yet demonstrate better character than those of us who say Jesus is the only way.

God is calling for real men and women of faith to come forth. Too many have been missing in action from God's army. Boot camp was too intense for them and so they stand outside the camp, looking in. They hope for the benefits of security and feel content in the liberty that God provided through His Son.

When I speak about Adam, the first man, dying, it is not man as in gender, it is man as in His created order. The world is not missing a man of God in gender, it is missing the creative order of God demonstrated through His creation. It is missing a woman who was created to be under the authority of man. Where do we find the real woman of God, full of the graces of God, who understands virtue, who will not be defiled by the serpent, who will be restored back to the place where God can bring glory? One who so resembles the model of Christ and is unlike the world that a sinner knows he cannot touch her?

God sent Jesus to earth because of Adam's fall and the prevailing diminishing standard. We are surrounded by people who call themselves people of God but continue to live by this diminished standard. God knew this and so He sent Jesus to become the perfect example of the absolute character of God.

Historians agree that Jesus lived on the earth. They may deny He was God, but they admit there was a man named

Jesus and they know through historical records that no fault could be found in Him. Even researchers of other religions will accept the premise that Jesus was a righteous and holy figure. Again, they will not admit He was God. No judge or attorney through past centuries could ever produce any evidence showing any fault found in Him. They recognize that He lived and died and rose again. But they fall short of the glory of honoring Him.

Man promotes what God has cursed. Just look at the television listings and notice the endless talk shows that present anybody who will boost their ratings. They spew out amoralism. They reach millions of people, offering sleaze and sensationalism. The ratings soar as the audience bows low to the god of lust.

God is looking for individuals described by Ezekiel,

So I sought for a man among them who would make a wall, and stand in the gap before Me on behalf of the land, that I should not destroy it; but I found no one.

Ezekiel 22:30

God displayed His great care for mankind. Even as Jerusalem had a wall around it to protect its people, so God wants to wall up His own, lest any should injure His vineyard. It was a hedge against unrighteousness—false doctrine—as seen in Proverbs 4:2: "For I give you good doctrine: Do not forsake my law." Corruptions had crept in.

God had shown these people good laws, purity in worship, and had given them good prophets, priests, and princes. They had opportunities and missed them because they answered the cry of their flesh instead of putting it to death. Jehoshaphat brought the people back from their idolatry and false doctrine and so the Lord God of their fathers became the hedge. God protected them. The Bible is filled with illustrations and warnings of how sin can breach walls.

In these last days, I thank God again for Promise Keepers who are seeking for men to stand in those gaps—men who hate sin and love God and want more out of their life. Men missing in action, started in the garden where it all began. But follow me and I'll show you something by chronicling the life of Eli who was a priest. Man misses this priestly order. He is missing in this relationship area and therefore everything else collapses. Revisit the home. Who in church families usually prays with the children? It is most often the woman. Who reads the Bible to the church? The woman. Who prays for the family and assists in the church? Most likely, the woman.

Man is filled with pride and finds it difficult to stand in the hedge at work. He fears the reproach of men and so is a silent witness that the living God has come into his heart. Why? Because he is not ruling as God intended. Man is being ruled by the influence of other men.

I see this in pastors. Many can be so influenced by men in this day that they may move across the country to answer the call of a bigger church even if they have not outserved God's purpose where they are. Man without God can be bought. If God is not ruling in your heart, then somebody else's vision is governing your life because you do not know the vision of God. You have abdicated your spiritual relationship with God. You are not a man at all. You run from becoming a part of the hedge and leave a gap open.

Eli was very old. He was at the door of the tabernacle of the congregation (1 Sam. 2:22). Eli's sons had conjured up abominable things. It is hard to recover from sexual sins. God hates sexual sins because the essence of our relationship with God is knowing Him. The spiritual union of our relationship with

Him is to produce spiritual children. Sexual sin violates our union with God and the Holy Spirit.

Eli's sons were exposed. That is what God does with sin. He brings it into the light of His holiness. I do not write this to be harsh or brittle. I am writing what God says in His Word. He searches for purified men who will not discount His glory or His honor.

The child Samuel grew up and was in favor with the Lord and men (1 Sam. 2:26). Amidst the ungodliness of Eli's sons, Samuel grew in the ways of the Lord. He matured with such a sense of God's backing that "none of his words were allowed to fall on the ground" (1 Sam. 3:19). The elders at the gate of the city would ask when he approached, "Are you coming peaceably?" Here is a picture of a man of God who, when he approached a city, was so honorable, word spread well in advance of his coming. His very word had the authority to remove a man from office. At the time Eli's sons, by sinning, were falling out of favor with God, someone else was being prepared to take their place. Someone else to stand in the gap. The very thought of God setting me aside strikes terror into my heart. But if I do not fulfill the will of the Lord, He already has another to step into my place, and there goes my right to be prepared to rule in the kingdom.

Eli's sons show us three things. They abdicated their responsibility as men of God. They misrepresented the character of God, and they lowered the standard of the office of the priesthood. The Word goes on to say, "And there came a man of God unto Eli . . . an old man in thy house" (1 Sam. 2:27–32). Does it amaze you that the Lord came to Eli rather than his sin-sick sons? The ones who were stealing from the offering brought to the temple? Men who were using God for their own advantage? God dealt with both the sons and the father because somewhere along the line the father had abdicated his spiritual responsibility before God and allowed generational sin to be seeded into the next generation.

What Eli needed was a sharpened awareness of God. He had allowed a misappropriation of God's standard, not only in his generation, but also in the next. He allowed the guilt of the people before the Lord to be slackened. In so doing, the whole ministry of being able to hear the voice of God was lowered. In those days, the people came to the priests for answers. Their answers were diluted by priests who were not hearing the voice of God and did not have the character and integrity to hear the voice of God.

Tragically, Eli lost his integrity. He lowered the standard. Part of the promises of a Promise Keeper deal with a man and his integrity. Some call it rigid. I praise God for godly standards. If God had not raised up Samuel to take Eli's place, the people would have been destroyed because there must be somebody who is innocent to stand for the guilty.

I am faithful only to God, and I remind the body of Christ what the Word of the Lord says: The sins of the fathers visit the third and fourth generation (Exod. 20:5). I want to sharpen your level of awareness in these critical issues. There are two levels of fathering. In the inner city of Los Angeles, drug-dealing is an epidemic. One of the tragedies is now finding three generations of drug dealers. The fathers have trained their sons to run drugs, and often second-generation fathers use their five- and six-year-old sons to watch out for the law. Already many sons have come to premature deaths because of their involvement with their fathers. Other's live on the sharp edge of existence because of the copycat sins of their fathers. This generational sin contributes to the destruction of a race whom God created. Drug lords respond that they have never forced anyone to sell for them. I doubt Eli made his sons commit sin with the women in the temple. But the principle has never changed. What a man sows, he reaps.

We tend to think that most of the drug dealers are black and forget there are many rich white-collar people who make drug deals costing millions of dollars. The responsibility is widely shared. It is scary to think God allows this to continue until some person finds God and lifts a standard of righteousness.

The same is true for men who ignore God and see gain unrighteously. God is not going to deal just with ghetto dwellers. He will deal with their financiers and the corrupt of this world. It holds true for doctors who are aborting children during the latter stages of pregnancy and still calling it a fetus. That is a child, formed and fashioned in the image of God. These doctors have been bought with money, but the children they abort have been bought with the precious blood of the risen Christ. It is a fearful thing to fall into the hands of the living God. The god of this world and the judgment of God will be upon them.

We see God's hand with Eli and how He deals with the sins of the fathers. It is even more abhorrent because Eli was a priest, a man with spiritual responsibility. Do you realize that today we are called a royal priesthood? The very essence of our being saved is that we can pray to God and know that He hears us. Yet we neglect the very act of prayer that draws us into the presence of God through Jesus. Our love for God is proven by prayer.

I am touched by Psalm 26:8: "LORD, I have loved the habitation of thy house." That means you have loved an inner sense of cleanliness because we are the house of God. The Bible says that our bodies are the temples of the Holy Spirit. How many people are you acquainted with who do not think much of themselves? How many Christians feel disconnected or discouraged? David wrote that he loved the habitation of God's house. We are God's house, so why not be elated? In His presence is fullness of joy and at His right hand pleasures forevermore (Ps. 16:11).

Something is missing if you do not love His house within you. Maybe you need some house cleaning. You should love and respect yourself when God reigns inside with you. We are one in Christ.

The house should become a house of prayer, of thanksgiving and praise. God inhabits the praise of His people. No wonder David loved the habitation of His house. It was a place where honor dwelled. Do you fall short of the glory or honor of God? Is your house one where character is developed? He does not look for earthly credentials, wealth, or prestige; He searches for character. Men missing in action today are those who are not modeling what the house of God should look like.

The garments of the priests were to be for glory and beauty as shown by Aaron in Exodus 28. Glory means honor. Aaron and his sons were dressed to the hilt. There was no substandard material at all because the garments represented the character of Christ. The garments were symbolic of glory and honor and the beauty of God; attributes that we are to show to a world that appears pretty unimpressed with Christians. If they see His beauty in you, you will attract them.

All That We Have Is the Lord's— We Give It Out of His Hand

Every nation has an ambassador, one who sharpens the awareness of other nations regarding his own nation. The Bible says that we are ambassadors for Christ. Many Christians do not understand that yet. They still think they are representing themselves. They perceive they hold title to their house, that their finances are theirs, but they ignore that they are being sustained by God. They are the explanation of God; they are here because of God and yet they think that what they have is theirs. I like the Dutch translation of the verse that relates "all that we have comes from the Lord and we give it out of His hand." That is viewing from the large to the small, seeing things from God's point of view.

The church needs a sharpened awareness of how money is handled. Your Swiss accounts can be burgeoning, but unless God is the God of your pocketbook, He says your pocket will ultimately be full of holes. The streets of heaven are paved with gold, and someday we will walk on them. Until we learn to walk on our money and to think little of it except in terms of what it can do to sustain us and build the kingdom, He still has work to do with our character. We are stewards of God with all of our resources.

At times I meditate on the memory of Moses. When reading this order, I notice the intricacy of the priesthood as described by him to Aaron and his sons. They could not forget one detail, and if they did, they were not given another chance. We say that this is the Old Testament or the Old Covenant. Some respond by saying, "You're too legalistic, Boone." No, I look at those people and their high level of commitment and wonder why our lives are not producing at least some of what theirs did.

We Americans pride ourselves on our independence. We live in a free nation. But it is just the opposite where God lives. God takes pride in His children's dependence. You are not the author or finisher, the alpha or the omega. Yet in our weakness, wickedness, and independence He has called us to Himself. He takes what we do not have and places Himself into us and wants to fill our house for time and eternity. We have the choice of independence or dependence. Of demanding our own rights or signing away our rights to Him. Either way, someday, "at the name of Jesus every knee should bow, of those who are in heaven, and on earth, and under the earth, and that every tongue should confess that Jesus Christ is Lord, to the glory of God the Father" (Phil. 2:10–11, NASB).

Is it not time to rally men who have been missing in action and all people of God who will say, with Oswald Chambers, "The passion of Christianity is that I deliberately sign away my own rights and become a bond-slave of Jesus Christ. Until I do that, I do not begin to be a saint"?

That is sharpening our awareness of God, who promised, "Behold, I will make thee a new sharp threshing instrument. . . . That they may see, and know, and consider, and understand together, that the hand of the LORD hath done this, and the Holy One of Israel hath created it" (Isa. 41:15, 20, KJV).

10

Feast of In-Gathering

And it shall come to pass, that every one that is left of all the nations which came against Jerusalem shall even go up from year to year to worship the King, the Lord of hosts, and to keep the feast of tabernacles. And it shall be, that whoso will not come up of all the families of the earth unto Jerusalem to worship the King, the Lord of hosts, even upon them shall be no rain. And if the family of Egypt go not up, and come not, that have no rain; there shall be the plague, wherewith the Lord will smite the heathen that come not up to keep the feast of tabernacles.

Zechariah 14:16–18, KJV

*T*he quest for God's truth is a lonely one indeed. There are times when I feel like John the Baptist, a voice crying in the wilderness of this present world, or Moses, in his intensity from God, pleading "Let my people go." Go where? Right straight to the heart of God, nonstop into the face of Jesus, breaking through into Christ's likeness.

We deplore slave owners, yet remain slaves of sin. Are the shackles that impede us from commitment and revival any less debilitating than those that bound our black ancestors on slave ships? The bondage of sin is more severe than the temporary loss of freedom. The consequences of sin and a life not right with God ends in damnation. Everything we do is about eternity.

There are multiple definitions of truth. The search is endless, which is why we must determine to stay solidly committed to the Word of God. Conditions described by Isaiah in his day bear remarkable similarity to our cities and inner cities.

And justice is turned back. And righteousness stands far away; for truth has stumbled in the street, and uprightness cannot enter.

Isaiah 59:14, NASB

Picture "truth," "justice," and "righteousness" as three people walking single file into a doorway. If Truth stumbles in the doorway, Justice is turned back. If Justice is turned back, Righteousness stands far away. This is precisely what is happening in America today. It was obvious to Isaiah that Truth needed to be lifted and released from its fallen position so Justice could reign, so Righteousness could enter the city.

Charles Spurgeon wrote that there are two "thirst creators" of life. They are love and sin. In the garden, Eve symbolized the eternal dissatisfaction sin creates in man. Jesus, on the other side, symbolized the eternal restlessness of love as it seeks to bless its object. Both seek satisfaction. Jesus said, "He satisfies the longing soul, and fills the hungry soul with goodness" (Ps. 107:9). Isaiah further wrote, "I will pour water upon him who is thirsty, and floods on the dry ground" (Isa. 44:3).

Portraits of Faith

Do you know the intentions of God in your life? The patriarch Abraham saw our day. He became heir to the promise. Here was an old man who left everything to follow the Lord. He had consecrated his life and family to the Lord and was conformed to the character of Christ. His was a lifestyle of faith, even to the point of solemn obedience in being willing to sacrifice his only son. He took his faith on that lonely walk up the mountain where the sacrifice of Isaac was to take place. As the two left the servant behind, Abraham told him, "We will be back." He knew God had provided the sacrifice. He had not questioned how. Why? His faith took him to the level of confidence that no matter the circumstance, whatever God says or requires is better. God, the self-existing one, the El Shaddai, was ever manifesting His presence.

Another breakthrough hero of the Bible was Moses. He was awesome. He had tried and failed in his own strength, but then he allowed God to lift him up to a higher dimension. He spent forty years on the backside of the mountain and chose to give up on Egypt and all that the world could offer so as to dedicate himself to the Lord. He feared Pharaoh until he experienced the burning bush and became a broken man. He accepted the demands of obedience and was willing to move, accompanied only by the presence of the Lord. God assured him, as He has every true believer, I will be with you. He had been tested and fled when he was strong. Now he was going back when he was weak. In his weakness God displayed His power.

Meekness Is Not Weakness but Strength Harnessed for Service

I love that man! I strive to live by his example. Meekness is not weakness; it is strength harnessed for service. That is the Lord. In that context, this man became the shepherd of Israel. He sharpened his awareness of God through fasting and devotion. I like Moses because he was not only a revivalist, but he obeyed God and delivered the nation.

His numerous, mighty adversaries numbered six hundred thousand. He was just one man with a stick. They were Green

Berets—the elite, representing their nation's best. He obeyed God and walked in His ways, and God made him credible in the eyes of the world and in the eyes of Israel.

He was humble and abased. There was no pride in him. He took no accolades when given the opportunity. He was prepared and put his life on the line for the people, even though most were disobedient. He, like Jesus, ate to sustain himself for the task, not just to fill his physical body.

Moses was not only a revivalist, he was a reformer. He became one of the faces of reconciliation for the nation. He brought law to the people as a revivalist and brought back the reality of the living God at the same time God was giving him the law. This was the basis of his intimacy with God. He was able to set up a structure on how society should be modeled. He modeled as a reformer.

Joseph is a magnificent portrait of a man who restricted society in preparation for famine. Joseph went through fourteen years of suffering. He was sold by his brothers, suffered the trials of being in Potiphar's house, and, because of a woman's unfounded accusations, went to prison. From a human perspective, everyone forgot about him, but God didn't. He lived on his dreams and the presence of God. He fed on the bread of his destiny. He would not compromise.

Joseph never lost faith and never blamed men. He went through the painful groundwork of worm training. When he was reacquainted with his brothers, he did not ascribe his circumstances to them. He ascribed them to God. He did what Jesus would do. He knew God meant it for good, and he blessed his brothers and fed them from the abundance of his house.

There are striking parallels between Joseph and Jesus. Joseph is called a type of the Son of God. He brings us into a clearer view of who Jesus is. Each, for a time, lived with his father. Jesus said, "I came forth from the Father, and am come into the world" (John 16:28, KJV). Joseph lived with his father and was greatly beloved. Each were objects of love and hate. One day our Lord was greatly exalted as He came into Jerusalem. Soon after, He was crucified between two malefactors. Joseph was sold for a few pieces of silver, and Judas betrayed Jesus for a mere thirty coins. Each was plotted against, one by his brothers and the other by so-called friends.

While on earth neither Jesus nor Joseph lost sight of their destiny, the original intent of the Father. Both, with unswerving allegiance and obedience, became exalted, one in the house of the Pharaoh in Egypt and the other at the right hand of God. Through their sufferings, crushed as worms, they were lifted up, and that suffering, rightly responded to, accomplished God's purposes.

Jesus and Joseph both prepared a place for their own. Even as Uncle Tom was mistreated and yet cared more for a lost sinner than for his own life, the color of character was once again painted with the brush strokes of humility and holiness.

Elisha gives yet another glimpse into the life of faith and power. He was relatively unknown in his time, yet his prayers stopped up the heavens and prevented any precipitation for three and a half years. We know nothing of his parentage, and Thisbe, the place from which he came, appears in no world atlas. He possessed no earthly portfolio or worldly credentials. He was not born to opportunity. He lived lowly, even as did his mentor, Elijah. There is no biblical sign an angel came to him with revelation, but he "knew":

As the Lord God of Israel liveth, before whom I stand, there shall not be dew nor rain after these years, but according to my word.

1 *Kings* 17:1

After the drought, the Lord sent him to revisit the palace where the pronouncement was first made. What gave him the courage to be so stubborn for God? Years before he had noted in Deuteronomy 11:16–17, "if you worship idols in this land that I have given you for a promise, I will shut up the heavens and not let it rain any more." God's word resided in his heart. This man, by himself, risked his life and stood up before a whole nation. Elisha risked, and in so doing introduced the real God. Let the true God of heaven be revealed by fire. He stood between God and the people. He steadfastly proclaimed that they were standing between two opinions. If God be God, serve Him. If not, keep Baal. No one came from the crowd to stand beside him and affirm him. But God's presence with him gave His approval. The only approval of merit in this short sojourn on earth was that God backed him up. When it became popular, safe, and comfortable, the people came back, too.

I love Peter because he was perceived by his peers as dumb. But this one who appeared "dumbed down" was lifted up as the mind of Christ was driven into him. He was presumptuous and had an entrepreneurial spirit of risk, willing to go all the way. I admire him because he came from menial means, identified as a fisherman from the wrong side of the tracks, and had an unimpressive background. But the Lord saw him and made him one of His big three.

Peter made mistakes. We see his weakness as he was around the fire with those who were mocking Jesus. He denied his Lord three times, saying he was not one of His followers. But from that point of denial he moved into the refining fire of repentance. He was correctable. The result? He caught the fire of Jesus and was willing to follow Him, even to death. This transpired after the outpouring of the Holy Spirit and took him to another level. I believe Peter most resembles a street guy for Jesus. With his "blade," he even cut off the ear of a Roman soldier who came to arrest Him. He took chances but learned from his mistakes. Should we not do the same?

Timothy was a disciple who loved learning and could carry out what Paul began. He was brilliant beyond his age and social level. He sucked up all the anointing Paul had and was blessed by a godly mother and grandmother who seeded the Word into him. He was focused. He was not distracted by ego-mania. He was used at an apostolic level. He ordained other pastors. He held with trust the deposit of the glory and the anointing of God and could stand in Paul's stead.

History relates the lives of the great revivalists and reform-ers—Jonathan Edwards, Augustine, George Whitefield, John Knox, John Wesley, John Bunyon, Martin Luther, Charles Finney, Arthur and Lewis Tappen, Daddy Seymour—real men who faced their nations for their God. Men who modeled extravagant obedience. Societies were affected as they made the people of their day aware of the principles of the Lord. Consecrated men who paid the price of worship and sacrifice with a deep sense of willingness, not just to succeed, but to exceed and prepare people for the coming kingdom of God.

A sixteenth-century Venetian artist, Titian, portrayed Prudence as a three-headed man. Each head represented a different phase of age. One was youth, facing the future. One a mature man, eyeing the present. The third was a wise old man, looking back at the past. Described as an allegory of prudence, over the three heads was a phrase: "From the example of the past, the man of the present acts prudently so as not to imperil the future."

These heroes of the faith live in my heart as an admonish-ment to live pure and holy today so I will not imperil the future being prepared for me and those who are serious about their future reign with God.

We are in the last move of God. I believe we are moving toward the Feast of Tabernacles. This is sometimes referred to as the Feast of In-Gatherings.

The Bible presents three great feasts to us, times when people in the Old and New Testaments celebrated significant events. In the Old Testament, some parts of the food were reserved for the priests and the rest for those who had in-gathering at the temple.

Passover was celebrated in remembrance of when the Hebrews put blood on their doorposts, so that God would pass over their homes when God destroyed all the firstborn in the land of Egypt. In the New Testament, it was during Passover that Jesus was crucified. He was the sacrificial Lamb of God who took away the sin of the world.

Pentecost was a feast of harvest, thanking God for provision. The early, serious Christians witnessed the outpouring of His spirit while in the city of Jerusalem to observe Pentecost. This transpired fifty days after Jesus' death and resembled a jubilee in the upper room.

The Feast of In-Gatherings was a monumental celebration, a time of reflecting on the years the Israelites spent in the wilderness before entering the Promised Land. In the Old Testament, people made primitive-type dwellings to remind them of the times their forefathers journeyed with Moses.

The Feast of In-Gatherings represents the table of the Lord for the church. It is used as a memorial and is prophetic; memorial in that it refers to the redemption of the people out of Egypt and prophetic as this relates to Israel after her restoration. It then becomes a feast for the church at large and also for the nations.

And it shall come to pass, that every one that is left of all the nations which came against Jerusalem shall even go up from year to year to worship the king, the LORD of hosts, and to keep the feast of tabernacles. . . . The LORD will smite the heathen that come not up to keep the feast of tabernacles. . . . And I heard a great voice out of heaven saying, Behold, the tabernacle of God is with men, and he will dwell with them, and they shall be his people, and God himself shall be with them, and be their God.

Zechariah 14:16, 18;
Revelation 21:3, KJV

This will be a great in-gathering where the church will make Jesus king, with all authority. The church will have become as one. Jesus will reign and rule all people. Denomination, color, creed, and gender will all dissolve into one family of God having achieved its destiny. All faces will be turned to Jesus, the express image of God, the picture-perfect face of reconciliation.

This last great Feast of Tabernacles portrays the recovering of the ark of the covenant. When David was king, he was determined to restore the ark to its rightful place. Saul had ignored this responsibility. The ark has always been symbolic of the presence of God.

At Mount Sinai, Moses experienced that only once a year could a man approach God. On Mount Zion, at the great in-gathering, the curtain will be flung wide open, and we will witness the presence of Jesus Himself. Jesus who pioneered the way for us. Passover was celebrated; Pentecost is being accomplished. Now, Lord, hasten the day and make us prepared for this great Feast of In-Gatherings. I pray His presence will dominate your lives and mine.

Nevertheless I am continually with thee; thou hast holded me by my right hand. Thou shalt guide me with thy counsel, and afterward receive me to glory.

Psalm 73:23–24, KJV

11

Eternal Focus

Teach me thy way, O Lord; I will walk in thy truth: unite my heart to fear thy name. I will praise thee, O Lord my God, with all my heart: and I will glorify thy name for evermore.

Psalm 86:11–12, KJV

I reflect back on my life and vividly remember crying out to God, "If You are there, God, I need You to reveal Yourself to me." I knew He was after me. Suddenly, the Shekhinah glory of God filled my room. I knew it was serious. Magnificently, He poured His living words into my life and being.

Thus saith the Lord that created thee, O Jacob, and he that formed thee, O Israel, Fear not: for I have redeemed thee, I have called thee by thy name [Wellington Boone], thou art mine. Since thou wast precious in my sight, thou hast been honourable, and I have loved thee: therefore will I give men for thee, and people for thy life. Fear not, for I am with thee: I will bring thy seed from the east, and gather thee from the west: I will say to the north, Give up, and to the south, Keep not back: bring my sons from far, and my daughters from the ends of the earth; even every one that is called by my name; for I have created him for my glory; I have formed him; yea, I have made him.

Isaiah 43:1, 4–7, KJV

Yes sir, Jesus! That is mine. Mine to appropriate as I seek to outserve and outhunger this world for God and present to the body of Christ the reality of Baal-Perazim. God being the God of breaking through. "So David went to Baal Perazim, and David defeated them there; and he said, 'The LORD has broken through my enemies before me, like a breakthrough of water.' Therefore he called the name of that place Baal Perazim" (2 Sam. 5:20).

"Teach me thy way, O LORD; I will walk in thy truth; unite my heart to fear thy name. I will praise thee, O Lord my God, with all my heart: and I will glorify thy name for evermore" (Ps. 86:11–12, KJV).

Appendix 1

I Have Called You by Name

But now thus saith the Lord that created thee, O Jacob, and he that formed thee, O Israel, Fear not: for I have redeemed thee, I have called thee by thy name; thou art mine.

Isaiah 43:1, KJV

Many of us have had defining moments in our lives, a time when God reached down and touched us, leaving His indelible prints on our life. It was such an event one night that changed my life forever. I have come to understand that God's center is everywhere and His circumference is nowhere. God proved this to me when He found me amidst the rubble and ruin of the ghetto and showed me what He can do with ruined things. He saw me when I was all-Europe in three sports. He saw me in Vietnam, a fearful mortar man on a hill surrounded by Viet Cong. He saw me in a floundering relationship with my father while I was living with my mother and her abusive, violent live-in. He saw everything that I ever was, but He focused on what He had ordained me to be. God became the only father I would truly know.

There was a time in my life when I was uncertain of my direction. It all came to a head one night. Yes, I was a Christian, but I didn't have a sense of purpose or calling. I began to have feelings but didn't understand them. Yet they were very real and powerful to me. It was as if God was forewarning me that He was about to do something in my life.

On this particular night I was having dinner with a friend.

Again I became confused. I knew the Lord was trying to reach me. I heard a sound in my consciousness. The woman with me was puzzled at my lack of focus as she watched me from across the table. The same sound came to me again. I was looking blankly at her, and she was looking back at me. Suddenly, in the midst of staring at each other, I abruptly said, "We have to stop this. God is calling me."

For the next few minutes everything we said to each other was unintelligible. She looked at me, stunned. Neither of us could make sense of the moment. It was as if we were sitting at the table of Babel. I stood up. She slowly rose to her feet and we disappeared into the night in opposite directions.

I returned to my room. In utter confusion I cried out to God. "God, if You are there, I need You to reveal Yourself to me." Again that same sound came into my mind. I felt desperate. I knew the hound of heaven was after me. I began to consider my life's purpose and value. This couldn't be all there was to the Christian life. There had to be more to it than this. "God, if You are there, I need You to reveal Yourself to me."

He was and He did.

As I lay stretched out on my bed, from nowhere and everywhere, the Shekhinah glory of God flooded my room. I was struck with terror. I had been fearful in Vietnam. That was serious. But when the glory and presence of the living God filled my room, I dared not move. I lay rigid on my bed overcome with the holy fear of God's presence.

If I Moved, the Glory of God Would Kill Me

Even though I couldn't move, I began to see myself. At first I was hyperventilating, then I was sprinting out of my shoes. All the while I felt that if I moved one fiber of my being, the glory of God would kill me. If I thought a bad thought, it would kill me. I couldn't move. I couldn't think. All I could do was stay stock-still in the trance. God did not say anything. He did not do anything. Yet I was assured His presence was there.

I don't know how long this lasted, but when His glory moved out of the room, I reached for a Bible at the head of my bed. It surprised me the Bible was still there. A Catholic girl had given it to me. Although not saved herself, she told me I was a sinner and needed the Bible. It makes me laugh every time I think that God used a non-Christian to give me a Bible. Don't ever forget: The Lord will use whomever He wants to accomplish his purposes.

I grabbed the Bible, and it fell open. I looked down, my eyes fixed on the living words of God,

But now, thus says the LORD, who created you, O Jacob, And He who formed you, O Israel: "Fear not, for I have redeemed you; I have called you by your name; You are Mine."

Isaiah 43:1

I already knew about redemption. But as I read, "I have called you by your name; You are Mine," somehow the glory of God in that room completely absorbed my heart. I cried out, "Thank you, Jesus. Thank you, Jesus," over and over again. I knew I was truly converted. I was saved. All over my being, I possessed joy unspeakable. I was instantly changed. I couldn't sleep. I couldn't believe what was happening. Was it some kind of out-of-body experience? Was I dreaming? No, it was as real as this book you are reading. Finally exhausted, I fell into a deep sleep. In the morning I knew I had been changed forever. That's how it is when God comes to touch you; you can never be the same again. I was on the verge of a new adventure with

Jesus Christ as my captain. I couldn't contain the joy. Up from my bed I jumped and shouted, "Yes sir, Jesus. This is it!"

When God Comes to Touch You, You Can Never Be the Same Again

The next move I made was for my Bible. I lunged into the Word of God. Normally meticulous in the way I dressed, I threw on clothes that didn't even match. There could be no distractions. Only Jesus. Everything I had previously loved lost its value. I turned everything loose. Jesus wanted all of me, and I wanted all of Him.

At the time, I was doing well by selling real estate. When I arrived at the office that morning, I told everyone what had happened. I went to each person and asked, "Do you know the Lord? Not about Him. Do you know Him? Is the Lord real to you like He is to me?" Two days later I gave up the job. I knew it was not for me.

I called Katheryn, who would later become my wife. We had been interested in each other, but she doubted that I was saved and committed to Christ. During our conversation I preached to her for an hour. I couldn't stop. She was numb. She couldn't believe it. In that hour the doubts were handled. Three months later we were married!

I started doing street evangelism. I would open the door of my car and set out barricades that would direct people to walk by where I was speaking. As they came, I would declare, "You must be born again. Jesus is coming soon." I did it over and over again. I did the same with pastors and others I met. I'd say, "Do you know Jesus, man? Do you really know him?" Often these guys would pat me on the back and say, "You'll be all right after a while."

I want to tell you, twenty-three years later, I am not "all

right." Many who knew me thought this was a passing fancy. They were and are still wrong. The Lord Jesus Christ touched my life and nothing else matters. He is Lord and He is coming back to claim His own. This is what helped me and kept me that transforming night when Jesus poured His glory into me. The Spirit of God jet-propelled me into the Word of God.

From that night it was clear that God had placed His mark on me. I was now completely His property. But why should God touch my life? Why did He reach out to me? Why did He show mercy to me? From a human standpoint, my life should have been a complete shambles. There were no silver spoons around my highchair.

My Mother Tried to Abort Me Several Times

In 1948 I was born to Rose Boone. She already had two other children and did not want another. After several failed attempts to abort me, I made it into the world. She lived "loose," and I was one of the results. From the start I was passed back and forth between relatives. Much of my childhood was spent with a grandmother and grandfather who lived in North Carolina and who had no control over me. When I was five years old I ran loose on the streets and stayed out until midnight. I didn't attend school. When I got into trouble, I would find a way to bring candy to my grandfather and had a way of sweet-talking my grandmother. Early on, I was learning to be a salesman!

I saw the inside of a schoolroom for the first time when I turned eight. Starting kindergarten at that age was embarrassing, but God had given me a good mind. In no time I skipped three grades. Soon I caught up with my peers.

By now I was moved back in with my mother and her boyfriend. He beat her every day. Neither this man nor my father—whom I met for the first time when I was thirty-five—

were married to my mother. When you violate God's law, the result is always ugly. Mother's live-in beat her so much. Many times I flew into a rage and tried to stop him. Then he would turn on me.

When you don't have God's protection you're on your own. Mother turned to sleeping with a kitchen knife for security. I was street-tough but still a little boy. Countless nights I lay awake in fear, wondering if that was the night she would use it. Mother carried that knife around and would often say, "I'll kill him when he goes to sleep tonight." The fear I had wasn't for her boyfriend. As a young boy, I hated him. I was worried for myself. If Mother killed him, she would be in jail and I would be put someplace else . . . again. For two years I lived in this atmosphere of violence. Every night as a little boy, stiff with fear, I stared at the bedroom ceiling wondering if mama would die or kill someone and I might be left alone.

I slept with the lights on. I wanted to stay close to where Mother was, but she would be with the men in her life. I remained a prisoner in the dungeon of my loneliness. To try to fill the void I would sneak out at night. Every night when I came home she would beat me with an extension cord. The same routine, night after night. She would make me strip and go through the ritual of taking her frustration out on me. I knew what the result would be before I went out every night, but I did it anyway. I lived in fear and grew up tough.

Living in Fear and Growing Up Tough

I was a streetwise country boy and told people I went to school so I could beat up other boys. The kids used to laugh at me, so I would have to fight my way in and out of school. Guys would jump me for no reason. I wanted to outjump them back. I was rough and wild. But I belonged to God even before I knew it.

He quickened my mind. I was blessed with a good memory. I didn't take notes in school, but would sit and listen. I passed the tests just by listening. I quickly moved ahead in school.

In 1958, Mother became very ill. Her heart rate went down to thirty-eight. The doctors said she would die. Some women from a church my grandfather had built drove her from Newark, New Jersey, to Clinton, North Carolina. She hung by a thread between life and death. They placed a nitroglycerin tablet under her tongue and settled in for the ten-hour drive. I was in the car. My eyes darted back and forth with the thought of her dying and my being left alone again. I hated every moment of that drive.

When we arrived in Clinton, they put her limp body into a room, and the women from church went to work. No, not to a job, but the hard work of intercessory prayer. They prayed and prayed and prayed and believed God. This woman of the world—my mother—they saw with the eyes of God.

Outside, I tried to ignore my fears by playing. But every few moments I'd run to the door and look through the key-hole to see my mother lying motionless on the table. They were still surrounding her with prayer. It seemed like forever. Back out I would go to play some more. I wondered what was really happening.

The next time I went to the keyhole things were different. There she was, quiet and still on the table, and suddenly she jumped up and shouted, "Thank you, Jesus!" She was totally healed. I saw the power of God through a keyhole. In Vietnam I witnessed foxhole conversions, but this experience was a key-hole conversion.

When God touches your life you want to get rid of the sin in your life. Immediately Mother knew she must leave the sin-ful relationship she was in. If he ever discovered where she was, he would kill her as he had threatened so many times.

My uncle quickly took us away to Baltimore. An aunt took us in. When the man learned where we were, he came and tried to take Mother back physically. Don't doubt it, there is a time to fight, just like it says in the Book of Ecclesiastes. Fortunately my uncle was present, and the two of them got into it. I can still pull the incident vividly up into my mind as I remember them wrestling on the floor. My uncle was victorious and managed to get my mother away from this crazy man. From that point on, her life was changed. She became a dedicated woman of God. She joined the Church of God in Christ.

At ten, I became a Christian also. Within two years I began teaching a Sunday school class in the same church. God had claimed me for His own. His hand was on me. From the age of ten to sixteen, I led as pure a life as I knew how to. I never went to movies, listened to secular records, never dated or kissed a girl. In fact, brace yourself, the first woman I kissed was my wife! We met in Germany.

Mother married, and her husband was in the military. We went from Fort Riley, Kansas, to Germany. It was a hard transition. Yet now I know, God's hand was upon me. I had been through many changes and seen a lot of the dark side of life. Her marriage was difficult for me to accept. I had never had a father, and even now Mother's husband was no father to me. She quickly got pregnant, and they had two children. I had been the only child, then everything changed. In fact, I found myself with four brothers.

I never had a male role model. My dependence had to be on the Lord Himself. I see now that He had a purpose in this "musical chairs" life I led. And I have to laud my mother, because prior to her remarriage, she worked two jobs, got off welfare, and became a hard-working Christian woman.

When I was sixteen, we were assigned to Europe for three

years. Again I was on my own, because I was sent to boarding school. The first place my stepfather was stationed had no English-speaking school. I went to school sixty kilometers away, sleeping in the former maid's quarters of a black family who were paid to watch over me. The second year I was in Frankfurt, then back to Bremerhaven with a white family who took looking after me very seriously. I was with my parents but certainly wasn't raised by them. I knew my mother loved me, but she was never trained to be a parent. She had been wild herself until the Lord came upon her. She was then on a course of learning to be responsible. There is a sixteen-year gap between my youngest brother and me. So when my current guardians started requiring me to be responsible, there were a few sparks, but God was teaching me.

I had a God-given advantage in that I was a natural athlete. In the inner city as a child, I played a hot game of stickball. We used rocks as balls. In high school in Germany, basketball, track, and football were my sports, but it was basketball that led to my meeting Katheryn. In many ways it was a done deal. I was the only black basketball player, and she was the only black cheerleader. I believe God set it up. It had to be God because the only things we had in common at the time were sports. I was the stepson of an absent stepfather; she was the daughter of the commanding officer of the base, a colonel. It took two years for her father to speak to me, but I had God on my side! Eventually I won him over, and when it happened, for the first time in my life, I received unconditional love. For the first time I had a man in my life to look up to—a role model.

I was still religious, yet sports gave me a degree of safe freedom I had not experienced before. I started living in the flesh. I loved the attention that came with being a star athlete. For the next nine years it was pretty much the same, walking in the flesh. I was a good guy but not seriously committed to God.

Thankfully, God in His omnipotence and mercy would not let me go. I have since learned that one of life's greatest discoveries is not that we have freedom, but that we have boundaries and limitations and opportunities to learn what we can do within them.

Sports gave me mentors and some opportunities to deal with the public in sports conferences and with fans. I made all-Europe in all three sports. I was a one-man track team in Bremerhaven and finished third in the all-Europe event by running multiple events—the 100- and 200-yard dashes, broad jump, and triple jump.

Of the eleven awards the school gave, as the lead athlete, I received eight. The affirmation helped shape my personality. Exposure in all of Europe was also an asset because travel in those countries, especially London, was like university training. Little did I realize at the time that God was preparing me to work with athletes for the rest of my life.

God had more good gifts in store for me. Katheryn had made a list, a purely physical description of what the man she would marry would look like. I always wore prescription sunglasses because my eyes had been hurt by some flash photography. These replaced the thick glasses I had worn before and gave me a valid reason to look cool. I don't know if it was the sunglasses, but somehow I passed Katheryn's test. She says I told her I loved her three days after we met, but she didn't believe me. Today I wonder what took me so long! Although we weren't dating, I wanted to take her out. She had an aura that drew me in and gave me a sense of belonging.

As I mentioned above, Katheryn's folks rejected me at first. But when my picture was all over the sports sections and plastered on billboards, they began to see me as someone other than the guy who was after their daughter. Even so, they didn't accept me for some time to come.

not as I was, but as God had ordained me to be and became a mentor to me. God was at work in eternity, timing my life with precision, though I was not always aware of His purposes or why things happened the way they did. Christianity is a journey, not a destination. I had many "you" turns and off- and on-ramps, but He knew my way.

After my discharge, I took an exam for the post office. My thought was to work during the day and attend college at night. I scored high on the test and gained five points for having been in the service. As it turned out, I went to the University of Baltimore during the day and worked the night shift at the post office. After a year, my uncle asked me if I would come to North Carolina and work with him in real estate.

Being undisciplined and with little motivation to finish school, I went. I got into making money and ego-tripping. I was moving farther and farther away from the reality of God in my life.

Katheryn remained in college. Her mother would not let her drop out. While I was totally focused on making money, the Lord was using Kay James, Tom Skinner, and other friends from Young Life to bring Katheryn to a serious commitment to Christ. These were real Christian friends who truly cared about her. I was a real black sheep and, as far as they were concerned, bad news for her.

The night that God touched me with His glory changed everything. I was in the Word and saying yes Sir to Jesus. I was committed. The Bible says that Jesus went into the wilderness to pray. I wanted to follow His example and went to the wilderness. I was determined to follow Him with my heart, soul, and mind. No one had to tell me to do that, but I was following Him all the way. If He did it, I was going to be right there with Him. When God touches you with His glory, you can't hide it from others. Soon the skeptics were seeing a real change in me.

In time I was licensed for the ministry after giving intense testimony to the pastor of the church I had joined, the African Methodist Episcopal Zion denomination.

In three months, my pastor had died. I married Katheryn and we relocated to Roanoke, Virginia. There we were close to the James and stayed there for two years. I went to work in sales and catapulted to the top quickly. Then an amazing thing happened to me in two different jobs. I became Jonah! As long as I was aboard, it looked like the ship was going down. I believe two companies went down because of me. I was working hard. I even won a cruise to Bermuda, a reward for being a top salesman. Katheryn and I had a great time in Bermuda, but on our return the manager informed me the company had gone out of business.

With my previous experience, I was offered another job as an assistant sales manager and was quickly promoted. In three months, I had a 97 percent closing rate. I was the only black but had learned the necessary principles. Then Jonah struck again! The office closed—the only one in a nationwide group. God wanted me to jump off the ship of business and get onto the dry land of the ministry and call people to repentance. It could have been discouraging but it was just another time to say, "Yes Sir, Jesus."

I had been attending Roanoke Institute of Biblical Studies, connected with Grace Church. There I began learning about a biblical world-view. This was during the early 1970s, a time when the energy crisis hit the United States and unemployment was high. Everything around us looked uncertain when we made a tentative move to Richmond. In my heart, I believed God wanted me to find a man to submit to, one who could be a mentor to me. I visited churches looking for that man. The Lord led me to F. H. Thompson, and I became his associate pastor. This Baptist church was the church of my wife's mother, the church we were married in. The godly pastor died after a year, and again God wanted me to move out into His ongoing plan.

I started an individual ministry on the radio, just on Sundays. We would get calls and responses. It appeared to be the medium where I could exercise the gifts and share the increasing knowledge God was giving me. The radio program then went daily. I received more calls. This led to my holding Friday night seminars at the local YMCA. A racially mixed crowd of hundreds attended.

As I was preaching the word of God on the radio, I would encourage those who were hungry for more to come to the Friday night study. People kept showing up! It was then I was convinced it is the word only that fills the emptiness within people. The seminar outgrew the facilities, and we moved to a Holiday Inn, then on to Petersburg, thirty-five miles from Richmond, for Thursday meetings. It was there God impressed me to start a church.

During this period, I was going through more changes. God always has more to do in you than through you. God had to remove from me the desire to be a visible evangelist. I had a burning passion to reach for the whole world. I believed in something massive for God. But I was still too full of myself.

The Lord took me to Hopewell, Virginia, a city known for its poverty. There He was again remodeling me, teaching me, and I started into the process of brokenness, dependence, contriteness, and humility. I had to strip off the extraneous, the fleshly stuff and the world-winning mentality. I went through what I teach today and still experience: Except a kernal of wheat fall into the earth and die, it cannot grow up again. I was into the early stages of worm training! (see chapter 2)

In sleepy little Hopewell, six men got together and paid our rent in advance to give us a head start in the church. All of the men were white. Among them was attorney John Deal, a dear friend to this day. At the time he was heavily in debt. When I told him the vision God had given me, how the glory of the Lord's presence and character filled my room and Isaiah 43 took residence in my life, he locked spirits with me. He and his wife had Katheryn and me in their home. They seeded into us. They loved us.

Within fourteen months after our marriage, Katheryn had delivered two babies, the first conceived on our honeymoon. They were both seven-month babies. It was crunch time and challenge time. If you've been there, you know raising kids who are only a few months apart is tough business. It was also a time of commitment in my life because God was teaching me to get in there with Katheryn. I didn't know how to nurture a baby, much less two. Having had no father and very little mothering, I missed out on some much needed training. The heavenly Father had to show me. I prayed that God would make me into the father I never had. How He answered that prayer! I was there for those kids and found great joy in helping and serving Katheryn. The honor I receive from that woman blows my mind. I will always cherish her for her seeding into the children who their daddy is.

In 1992, my good friend Mark Arnold invited me to join him and work on a doctorate together. It was an inviting prospect, but the Lord said a firm no. He was showing me that He wanted to prove to me that my service was not to be one of might nor my power of studying and letters—I was to be led by His Spirit alone. There was a time when I wanted a degree badly—and let me say, I don't think there is a thing wrong with that—but God made it clear, I was not to seek earthly credentials. My university was from above and my textbook was the Bible. When people indicate they want to follow in my footsteps and be with me in the work, I must remind them there is a price to pay in praying, fasting, studying the Word, and denying the carnality of self while constantly seeking God's guidance.

I am surrounded by a great staff who are learned and hold many degrees. Most of my friends have impressive educational credentials. Most have been in the top echelon of their classes. I have been set apart to pass by this area of life. God did meet me some time ago and allowed me to stop being insecure about it. I know I am to be dependent on Him alone. It is what He requires of me.

As we progressed on building our first church, it was John Deal who stood with me. He offered to do the legal work for us as we established the Living Word Evangelistic Association. He personally gave me the first $250 to break ground and has done all my legal work up to the present time. He was rock-solid for me when we birthed another church in Ettrick, Virginia. Again he helped us financially, and he spoke the truth and said that someday I would reach a vast group of people. Praise God for the encouragement He brings us through His humble servants.

John Deal was building and expressing the vision of God in a black man for the glory of God. I have discovered that behind many black institutions and advancements are those of another color who have become an inspiration of activism by putting the love of God into action.

I serve a God of the past, the present, and the future. I am here for God. His glory has never departed from me since that life-defining day when His presence and glory flooded my room, my body, my soul, and my spirit. He has allowed me in these ensuing years to raise a family and raise up many ministries. I have been privileged to raise an awareness of a needed view of the kingdom of God and His righteousness, all the while going lower and lower. I've had to learn, sometimes painfully, that He shares none of His glory.

Isaiah 43:1 remains my touchstone:

Thus says the LORD who created you, O Jacob, And He who formed you, O Israel: "Fear not, for I have redeemed you; I have called you by your name; You are mine."

Can you hear God calling you by your name? Has He been calling you to total devotion to Him? Are you willing to find out what that means? Jesus Christ is looking for a man or a woman who will stand up and say, "Yes sir, Jesus!"

Are you ready? If so, then let your worm training begin!

Appendix 2

Resolution on Racial Reconciliation on the 150th Anniversary of the Southern Baptist Convention

WHEREAS, Since its founding in 1845, the Southern Baptist Convention has been an effective instrument of God in missions, evangelism, and social ministries; and

WHEREAS, The scriptures teach that "Eve is the mother of all living" (Genesis 3:20), and that "God shows no partiality, but in every nation whoever fears him and works righteousness is accepted by him" (Acts 10:34–35), and that God has "made from one blood every nation of men to dwell on the face of the earth" (Acts 17:26); and

WHEREAS, Our relationship to African-Americans has been hindered from the beginning by the role that slavery played in the formation of the Southern Baptist Convention; and

WHEREAS, Many of our Southern Baptist forebears defended the "right" to own slaves, and either participated in, supported, or acquiesced in the particularly inhumane nature of American slavery; and

WHEREAS, In later years Southern Baptists failed, in many cases, to support, and in some cases opposed, legitimate initiatives to secure the civil rights of African-Americans; and

WHEREAS, Racism has led to discrimination, oppression, injustice, and violence, both in the Civil War and throughout the history of our nation; and

WHEREAS, Racism has divided the body of Christ and Southern Baptists in particular, and separated us from our African-American brothers and sisters; and

WHEREAS, Many of our congregations have intentionally and/or unintentionally excluded African-Americans from worship, membership, and leadership; and

WHEREAS, Racism profoundly distorts our understanding of Christian morality, leading some Southern Baptists to believe that racial prejudice and discrimination are compatible with the Gospel; and

WHEREAS, Jesus performed the ministry of reconciliation to restore sinners to a right relationship with the Heavenly Father, and to establish right relations among all human beings, especially within the family of faith.

Therefore, be it RESOLVED, that we, the messengers to the Sesquicentennial meeting of the Southern Baptist Convention, assembled in Atlanta, Georgia, June 20–22, 1995, unwaveringly denounce racism, in all its forms, as deplorable sin; and

Be it further RESOLVED, that we affirm the Bible's teaching that every human life is sacred, and is of equal and immeasurable worth, made in God's image, regardless of race or ethnicity (Genesis 1:27), and that, with respect to salvation through Christ, "There is neither Jew nor Greek, there is neither slave nor free, there is neither male nor female, for [we] are all one in Christ Jesus" (Galatians 3:28); and

Be it further RESOLVED, that we lament and repudiate historic acts of evil such as slavery from which we continue to reap a bitter harvest, and we recognize that the racism which yet plagues our culture today is inextricably tied to the past; and

Be it further RESOLVED, that we apologize to all African-Americans for condoning and/or perpetuating individual and systemic racism in our lifetime; and we genuinely repent of racism of which we have been guilty, whether consciously (Psalm 19:13) or unconsciously (Leviticus 4:27); and

Be it further RESOLVED, that we ask forgiveness from our African-American brothers and sisters, acknowledging that our own healing is at stake; and

Be it further RESOLVED, that we hereby commit ourselves to eradicate racism in all its forms from Southern Baptist life and ministry; and

Be it further RESOLVED, that we commit ourselves to being "doers of the Word" (James 1:22) by pursuing racial reconciliation in all our relationships, especially with our brothers and sisters in Christ (1 John 2:6), to the end that our light would so shine before others, "that they may see [our] good works and glorify [our] Father in heaven" (Matthew 5:16); and

Be it finally RESOLVED, that we pledge our commitment to the Great Commission task of making disciples of all peoples (Matthew 28:19), confessing that in the church God is calling together one people from every tribe and nation (Revelation 5:9), and proclaiming that the Gospel of our Lord Jesus Christ is the only certain and sufficient ground upon which redeemed persons will stand together in restored family union as joint-heirs with Christ (Romans 8:17).

Assemblies of God
Resolution 25, Revised, Use of Black Ministries

WHEREAS, The Gospel of Jesus Christ declares God so loved the world, He gave his only begotten Son, that whosoever believeth in Him should not perish, but have everlasting life; and

WHEREAS, The Scriptures have promised that in the last days God would pour out His Spirit upon all flesh; and

WHEREAS, The world for whom Jesus died and the flesh upon which the Spirit is poured out is without regard to ethnicity, class, economic distinction, or gender; and

WHEREAS, The foremost exemplary model of Pentecostal community in the 20th century is the Azusa Revival where leadership and people joined together without regard to ethnicity, providing a divine rebuke against the Jim Crow laws and racial discrimination of this worldly age and throwing a shining light of God's intention for His church where the blood of Christ washes out the color line; and

WHEREAS, Because of the deep stain and sin of racism following the Azusa Revival, predominately black and white Pentecostal denominations went their separate ways for a season; and

WHEREAS, The Assemblies of God was established during that time of separation so that our Fellowship became one from which black persons were mostly absent; and

WHEREAS, Our testimony to the world has suffered as a result of this separation and our Fellowship has been deprived of the rich blessings which could have been made by our black brothers and sisters; and

WHEREAS, In the goodness of the Lord and in the fullness of time, the Holy Spirit prompted us as a body in our 1989 General Council to repent of and denounce racism as a sin; and

WHEREAS, Across this Fellowship congregations are opening their hearts to become multi-ethnic communities which bear witness to Jesus Christ who told us that the world will know us by our love for one another; and

WHEREAS, It is right that we repent of racism and ask our black brothers and sisters for forgiveness for failing to keep and treasure the shining ideal of Jesus and the 20th-century Azusa Revival; and

WHEREAS, We are committed to removing every last vestige of racism from our midst and restoring to the work of the Lord the blessing of an integrated Fellowship; and

WHEREAS, Toward this end we encourage from our hearts the full participation of black persons within the Assemblies of God in fellowship and leadership; and

WHEREAS, Action by this General Council is needed to give impetus to our districts, ministers, and people for the full inclusion of black brothers and sisters throughout our Fellowship; therefore be it

RESOLVED, That this General Council ask the general superintendent and Board of Administration, the executive and general presbyteries, the executive officers and presbyteries of districts, pastors and ministers, local church boards and congregations to take whatever actions are necessary or advisable to enhance and accelerate the progress being made in our Fellowship for the inclusion of black brothers and sisters throughout every aspect of the Assemblies of God; and, be it further

RESOLVED, That this Council request the general superintendent to issue a public statement speaking to the spirit of this resolution before the Council adjourns.

Appendix 3

Blessed Beyond Measure
Devotion Guide

Foundational Scriptures: Deut. 28:47; Eph. 3:20–21

We have come to see blessing as a mentality, a way of thinking. When we know we are blessed, we have hope for the future. We have vision. We have the affirmation of God. Blessed beyond measure is a point of demarcation, a step toward fulfilling our destiny. Developing our position based on our relationship with God: If we think our position is dependent on our relationship with men, we will compromise, as people do in politics. When we know God, we do not look anxiously about us.

1. Read eight chapters of the Bible. This is a time in which God desires to restore us back to His Word. We are responding to His directive.

Eight is the number for new beginnings. Every day is a new beginning in God, so every day we read another eight chapters. Listen to the entire New Testament on tape.

Key Scriptures: Isa. 28:10–11; 1 Cor. 2:13–14

A. Read at least eight chapters of the Bible daily; any one or more chapters from each of the eight different sections of Scripture that are specified below. This is a total of approximately 240 chapters a month.

The Holy Spirit will organize and synthesize your reading. It need not necessarily be topical. Just let the Holy Spirit give it a flow. Do not try to put topics together. Seek the Lord.

- The Pentateuch: Genesis, Exodus, Leviticus, Numbers, Deuteronomy
- The Historical Books: Joshua, Judges, Ruth, 1 Samuel, 2 Samuel, 1 Kings, 2 Kings, 1 Chronicles, 2 Chronicles, Ezra, Nehemiah, Esther, Acts

- The Poetical Books: Job, Psalms, Ecclesiastes, Song of Solomon
- The Book of Wisdom: Proverbs
- Books of the Prophets: Isaiah, Jeremiah, Lamentations, Ezekiel, Hosea, Joel, Amos, Obadiah, Jonah, Micah, Nahum, Habakkuk, Zephaniah, Haggai, Zechariah, Malachi
- The Gospels: Matthew, Mark, Luke, John
- The Epistles: Romans, 1 Corinthians, 2 Corinthians, Galatians, Ephesians, Philippians, Colossians, 1 Thessalonians, 2 Thessalonians, 1 Timothy, 2 Timothy, Titus, Philemon, Hebrews, James, 1 Peter, 2 Peter, 1 John, 2 John, 3 John, Jude
- Books on the End Times: Revelation, Daniel

Each day read one chapter from each of the eight categories listed above.

Remember this point of emphasis: This is not a through-the-Bible program to read the Bible in a year's time. Although systematic study does have its place, the goal of this exercise is to hear from God. We are not looking for something to do by rote or logic because we recognize the weakness of our own minds. We are learning to listen to the Holy Spirit so that we can develop a new level of creativity. True creativity comes from God. It does not come through the logic of our own minds. Logic assumes that everything about God is measurable, predictable, and understandable. But if you can measure something, that something cannot be God. His workings are immeasurable.

This should be your own personal, random reading of a chapter from each of these eight sections. We are trusting the Holy Spirit to give us a harmony of revelation that relates to us personally and corporately. We are looking for divine insight from God through the Holy Spirit, trusting Him to give us what is needed. Through this process, I want these Scriptures to become a reality.

Isaiah 28:10–11. In this discussion of the basics needed for faith, notice not only the mention of "precept upon precept, line upon line," but especially the words "here a little, there a little."